THE INDIA THAT IS INDIA

Owing to the antiquity and rarity of this book, certain pages are regrettably absent, and readability is compromised due to the blurring of the original text. If you possess any insights regarding the availability of these missing sections, kindly inform us. Your assistance is crucial in ensuring the completion of this significant work for the benefit of future generations.

THE INDIA THAT IS INDIA

ELIZABETH SHARPE

GYAN

Published by

GYAN

Gyan Publishing House
5, Ansari Road
Daryaganj, New Delhi-110002
Phone: 011-47034999, 9811692060
E-mail: books@gyanbooks.com

Distribution Network
gyanbooks.com
India, USA, Canada, UK, Australia

ISBN: 978-93-7225-336-8 (PB)

First Published, 1934

2nd Impression 2025

Printed at: Gyan Press, Delhi.

THE INDIA THAT IS INDIA
Author: ELIZABETH SHARPE

THE INDIA THAT IS INDIA

By

ELIZABETH SHARPE
KAISAR-I-HIND MEDALLIST
F.R.G.S., F.R.E.S., M.R.A.S., F.B.E.E., etc.

LONDON
LUZAC & CO.
46 GREAT RUSSELL STREET, W.C. 1
1934

DEDICATED TO

CAPTAIN ARTHUR JOHN DUDLEY-LAVENDER

IN EVER LOVING REMEMBRANCE.

To that which was written by his old friend, A. Babington, Esquire, an old Etonian and one of the most talented of writers and poets (in the leaderette of his paper, *The Daily Post*,[1] Bangalore), the writer can add no more—

"The late Captain Arthur John Lavender was only thirty-eight years of age, having been born on May 4th, 1889. His lamented death, by a melancholy coincidence thus occurred on his thirty-eighth birthday. The recital of his useful services is entirely inadequate to afford any idea of his merits and universal popularity. And he was popular not only because he was courteous to all, and considerate to the humblest of those with whom he came in contact. He did more than that. If the late Captain Lavender, within his modest sphere of action, could help a lame dog over a stile he would do so—and did so—often at considerable personal sacrifice. And yet he was one of the least self-assertive of men : quiet—even reserved —but he was ever out to help others, and that is perhaps as honourable and lovable an epitaph as any man can carry with him when he leaves this world.

It is no mere form of speech to say this: his early death will cause wide-spread sorrow in Bangalore. He was a personal friend of many years—he was everybody's friend—and notwithstanding his retiring nature, it will be long before he is forgotten in Bangalore. More prominent men go to their rest with infinitely less real mourning, and the tributes which are laid upon his last resting place will be very real tokens of affection."

[1] *The Daily Post*—4th May, 1927.

CONTENTS

LIST OF CHAPTERS

Many of these articles have been published in the *Illustrated Weekly* of India; some in the *World* of New York. All have been revised, and in many cases completely rewritten; but to the Editors of these papers, I am deeply indebted for courteous permission to reprint them in book-form.

E. S.

AUTHOR'S FOREWORD

To write a book about India and Indians is no easy task even for one who has lived amongst them, as the writer has, for 24 years.

These articles were written of India, and Indians, to prevent Europeans applying their own standards of judgment in solving problems which are essentially matters for the Eastern people alone. What the Western world itself feels about the matter is not the criterion best suited for a balanced judgment.

The views expressed here are not necessarily those of the author. But nothing has been exaggerated, and the descriptions and incidents may well be counted as part of the author's own experience.

CHAPTER I

The Purdah

WHEN one considers the mystery that has always hung round zenanas, the many strange tales, that the Western world holds as fact, are not wholly inexplicable.

The unknown holds romance: and romance is the breeding place of fiction. And yet there is no mystery. Zenanas in India contain women as happy and satisfied as Western women; in many cases happier, and far more contented. One is not prepared to say that there are no unhappy inmates of a zenana, for unhappiness is part of the lot of earthly mortals; but this much is certain: there is no more unhappiness in zenanas than there is in the palaces of Europe.

There is coming into existence a new type of zenana lady—still in the minority at present—one who has had her limitations pushed home very forcibly, but not always discreetly, by European women. This new type would like the fully fledged wings of her English sister, not realising that our highly bred women are as bound by rules and conventions as rigid as ever bound a woman of the zenana.

The new movement in India, that is bringing the Princes to realise the benefit of education for their wives and daughters on up-to-date lines, would gain added force if the right kind of Englishwoman as teacher or companion could always be procured: the kind who would sink some of her preconceived ideas about zenana life, and concern herself with grafting on the original tree, instead of wanting to uproot and plant without consideration. Could some of these well-meaning, but ill-advised, ladies realise to what lengths their indiscretion led them, they would certainly pause before they gave effect to their utterances.

It would rather surprise them to learn that the " pathetic interest " that, according to some of them, these " poor purdah prisoners " take in the outside world is only strongly developed woman's curiosity. The visit of an Englishwoman in the zenana is a novel event. The European hats alone are subjects for them to laugh over for hours together. (And, surely, in comparison to the pretty head-dress of the Indian zenana lady, some of our hats are as startling as they are ludicrous.)

Then again, the visit of an Englishwoman means dressing up in finest garments : donning beautiful jewellery and listening complacently to admiring comments. All the Englishwoman wears, and all she says, is gone over again with their husbands, brothers, relations and friends, not always accurately.

These well-meaning sympathisers do not know that the zenana prisoners (*sic*) hold their own courts, hear lectures of priests, and listen to the songs of poets and bards through latticed windows : and have their friends and relations to stay with them for months, and even years, at their pleasure.

Their one deprivation, and to most of them it is not a deprivation, is that they must not show their faces or persons to strange men. Here the writer speaks in all diffidence, knowing well that there are as chaste women in the zenanas of India, as in any court of Europe ; yet in tradition and custom, there is no friendship between the sexes in India: no transitory stages. The man becomes the possessor, the woman the possessed, within an hour's acquaintance.

In a country of hot and quick passions, could not that zenana system be much more a protection than a prison to a woman?

Another point which must not be overlooked is that the greatest advocates of the zenana are women themselves.

When a Maharani seeks a daughter-in-law for her son, the young Maharaja, she invariably chooses her from a zenana family.

These and similar remarks have often been heard by the writer: "I don't want a daughter-in-law who shows her face and form to men like the common women do."

Is it worth while discussing sentiment here, and possibly offend all the sentimentalists by saying that love (or hatred) is mostly a question of propinquity?

A rather charming Indian girl once informed the writer that the marriages of the Western world were most often the closing chapter of romance, whilst with the Eastern world it was the opening.

One wonders if she was wholly wrong.

Mutual antipathy is not confined to the East. These ignored women, using the word in a general sense; ignored for want of charm, beauty or culture, would be rather wretched old maids in Europe. In India they have a home and often children; and though they may not retain their husbands' love or esteem, they have a definite position.

Pity is a great quality; but there are certainly more deserving objects.

The lot of the high-caste Indian widow is terribly sad : but is it more so than the lot of any other real widow ? This particular reference is to zenana widows, the widows of princes, not the poor, suffering widows of those other orthodox classes. The writer sees the little round of life still going on placidly enough, without the loved face that makes all the difference between she who was once "the fortunate one" and is now "the ill-omened one."

The mother of the present Maharaja of Jodhpur, who was a princess of Bundi-Kotah, had a considerable amount of freedom even after she became a widow. She travelled, extensively, in her zenana saloon, and died in Jamnagar.

Her co-wife, a princess of Udaipur, the premier Rajput State in India, has, by her own wish, never left the fort since her widowhood : and even in her husband's lifetime, to leave the fort was against all her Rajput principles. On one occasion, during the visit of Colonel Sir Alexander Pinhey, who was then Agent to the Governor General in Rajputana, her husband, Maharaja Sirdar Singh sent for her to his palace on the plains to see some performance. She came in a carriage, swathed all round with thick curtains : the air coming in only from an opening underneath : came unwillingly, for she hated the comparatively open zenana of the modern palace below the fort. The strict seclusion of the fort was home and happiness to this daughter of the highest Rajput aristocrat.

One can judge by this incident alone the absurdity of saying that these great ladies are locked up without any consideration given to their wishes. In the Bengal of to-day, wealthy ladies of the Vaisya class, are taking to purdah of their own accord, feeling that it gives prestige.

CHAPTER II

A Day in an Indian Princess's Life

A SKETCH, for the benefit of the uninitiated, of the foundation on which zenana family life is built, will give the reader some idea of the family life of a Hindu. The joint-family system is seen in the zenana in its completeness: the mother—sometimes the grandmother—of the ruling prince, various widows of defunct brothers or uncles of the Maharaja; the maharanis proper, wives of the ruling prince; their daughters and daughters-in-law, are all together.

Age carries with precedence unusual dignities: though, like all the good things of the world, the abuse of this right has now led to a diminution, that, in many respects, is to be deplored.

The daughters-in-law of orthodox zenanas are obliged by custom to respect and comply with the wishes of their husband's relations from their mothers-in-law downwards, and any mistake committed here is considered an insult to the husband himself.

The daughters have a freer time: for in their father's house, they are considered sacred trusts for some other family. Rigid etiquette awaits them after marriage: till then they lead, in every respect, a practically untrammelled life: a life that is undoubtedly a pampered one, and hardly a fit training for the one to follow; yet they seem to make few mistakes, and all fall in with the routine expected of them very easily.

It is not that intrigue is part of their nature: but it is their business in life to know, not only how to please, but how to retain superiority in their own little wake of life. Sometimes these efforts are harmless enough: but there are undoubtedly occasions when they get out of bounds and are not so harmless: then one sees a nature that can only count as complete happiness the retaining of affection to the exclusion of all others.

The zenana lady has often found it fatal to arouse interest in any other person outside herself: that it is to her advantage to prevent or kill any unusual interest outside that which is included in her own. Even the modern zenana lady, whose trend of thought has been anglicised, has found this a useful rule.

The Indian girl is very different to her English sister, with strange undercurrents of feeling that are totally alien to the simpler English girl.

The plurality of wives in the zenana, with its incessant struggle for hold of a place, if not one of superiority at least of equality: a struggle in which even the children are forced to join, is, no doubt, one of the reasons of this difference in outlook.

Though, again, the question of co-wives is a subject to be approached from quite a different standpoint to that usually taken by the Western world.

A certain amount of physical jealousy undoubtedly prevails, but the moral degradation felt by the Western woman, in similar circumstances, is completely absent.

A concrete instance proving this fact: it is not uncommon for the non-favourite queens of a Maharaja to combine together in lessening the love or influence held by the favourite. They get the Maharaja to remarry; and should this occur to the detriment of the favourite, their joy at having succeeded in ousting her from his affections, considerably outweighs any grief at having still another person to share in their privileges.

This may appear a strange paradox: but anyone who knows intimately anything of zenana life will testify to its verity.

Western standards of happiness, unhappiness, are not the appropriate ones for judging the happiness, or unhappiness, of the East.

The Indian lady, in her own way, is, on an average, far happier than the more independent Western woman. Indeed, she openly pities her for several things which in themselves are no deprivation to the woman of the West, but would be so to the woman of the East: the Englishwoman's comparative scantiness of jewellery, even her much boasted freedom, are to the Indian lady evidence alike of the little value in which a Western woman is held by her parents or husband.

The non-existence of the joint family system in Europe is put down to complete want of natural affection.

The very things that have aroused the most pity are often the most treasured things of the East, where the absence of them has, in turn, aroused criticism and pity towards the Western world.

The Indian princess is supposed to rise early, bathe and sit for prayers: if she is married, she must go the round of the zenana, and pay her respects to her elders.

After doing this, she may break her fast. Later, the priest of the family comes to read a religious book behind latticed windows: or, for those who like it better, the dancing girls come to sing or dance.

This listening to a priest where the ladies sit unseen, seeing all, behind a latticed window, is purely perfunctory: some of the sober-minded listen, occasionally, in between the conversation of the younger and more frivolous, who, if they come at all, carry on a whispered conversation amongst themselves, quite undeterred by any solemnity of theme, finding the gossip of friends, or servants fresh from the bazaar, more entertaining.

The servant of the zenana is a privileged person. Past mistresses in the art of intrigue, some of them have worked untold harm in the zenanas.

Modern education has decreased her power which was at one time almost unlimited. A vivid reminder of a servant's misused influence over her mistress occurs in the tale of Kaikiyi, wife of King Dasarath, in the Ramayana: and in modern times, the writer knows of an instance where the Maharaja bade his wife choose between him or the dismissal of a favourite servant, and the Maharani made her choice in favour of the servant.

It is due to these servants that zenana ladies, through their latticed windows, know by name and appearance every servant of the State, male or female. Powers of observation, which one might expect to be blunted by a life of seclusion, are extraordinarily keen.

The zenana lady is far from being an ignoramus, even though her book qualifications may be limited.

She is more often than not a shrewd business woman with a natural bent for ruling, and a special aptitude for adapting herself to circumstances and holding her own.

Meals are served in different rooms, even from different kitchens, to give suitable facilities to those favoured ladies of the household whose husbands take their meals with them: or to those others who are orthodox, and require food cooked in Brahmin fashion.

The etiquette of the zenana is very strict. The father-in-law may never meet his daughters-in-law: though, oddly enough, a mother-in-law often meets and converses with her sons-in-law: a brother may never meet his younger brothers' wives.

This means that in a family of four brothers, the youngest may meet all his brothers' wives: the third all but the fourth brother's wife: the second only his elder brother's wife, and the eldest brother meet none of his sisters-in-law.

After meals, most zenana ladies have a siesta, sleeping away the hottest part of the day. Many of them have learnt to have afternoon tea after the siesta: but it does not hold the sway over them as it does over the European.

Zenana princesses have not yet learnt to smoke cigarettes:[1] though many of the older type of Mahomedan Begums have a decided weakness for "hobble-gobbles."

One, whom the writer knew personally, was never without her "hookah," and used to spend most of her time—when she was not eating or sleeping—in puffing at it, in between playing bezique.

Zenana ladies love cards; and play bezique, and a kind of whist splendidly. They haven't yet mastered bridge;[1] but when they do, their long memories, especially where cards are concerned, will make them the champion bridge-players of the world.

[1] This was written in 1919.

In the evening, the wives of the State officials arrive, each according to her status in modern motors, double-horsed carriages with drawn curtains, single-horsed carriages, or in gaily painted "shigrams" drawn by bullocks, completely covered by red cloth; and pay their respects to the ladies of the zenana.

A pleasant hour or more is spent in gossip. Often they dance together—old and young alike, like children—forming a ring; touching hands, bowing, pivoting and singing in unison, following the lilt of a single leader; while a maid-servant, in the centre, beats a drum with fingers rigidly stretched to exact out of a skin-covered drum its most penetrating sound, joining, herself, in the chorus.

As the sun wanes, a light is brought in. It is of the most simple kind, a wick made of twisted cotton, in an earthenware receptacle of ghee; this light is the signal for the lighting of every other lamp in the palace: all stand or bow, as the light comes in, making respectful salutations; the unmarried girls cracking their knuckles on the forehead, the married ladies prostrating, first to the queens, and then the elders: a pretty custom worth preserving.

This is the signal for the guests to depart, and the ladies of the zenana to go to their several apartments to adorn themselves for the night.

For Indian ladies of the zenana like the English-women dress in their best at night, when for the former their men-folk usually arrive.

These are they for whom the Western world spends its vain pity and sheds its mawkish tears! Not perhaps a full life, nor one used in its best sense: but certainly not an unhappy one.

Is not unhappiness a thing of decree measured only by one's capacity for enjoyment?

Yet there are they who would make a grievance for these contented zenana ladies who do not consider the home that protects them the prison that the Western world calls it in its ignorance.

CHAPTER III

POLYGAMY[1]

NO doubt the King and Queen of Afghanistan in attempting to remove by law the evils of polygamy—and they are many—made a very plucky attempt to bring Asiatic countries to the European way of thinking on this subject. But whether they were wise or not, the future will tell. For there is the Asiatic side of the question: certain evils that are attendant, in Asiatic lands, on enforced monogramy.

Both in India and Afghanistan, marriages are still those of convenience.

In the case of the daughters of a Maharaja, it is incumbent on their dignity to marry a Maharaja, or, at least, an heir-apparent. When there are many daughters, and the Maharajas and their direct heirs are few in comparison; when social opinion is so strong, the marriage market becomes tight.

Indians, with a few noble exceptions, have not, yet, reached a level of thought that views the non-marriage of their daughters with equanimity. A grown up unmarried daughter in the house is considered a stigma on the fair name of the parents. Rich or poor, or even diseased, an

[1] This was written when King Amanullah and Queen Souriya were still on the throne of Afghanistan. The writer's views, not necessarily her own were asked for in this matter.

Indian woman must be given in matrimony: and money is often poured out to secure a favourable marriage with one unfit for marriage.

Monogamy enforced must demand a selection as careful and as considered as possible, lest the nation degenerate to a degree beyond redemption.

It is still tacitly understood amongst a certain cultured class, the cream of India, that a second wife, if the first be satisfactory and able to bear children, is wrong. But if the wife, however charming, bears no child, the need of a son to a Hindu, being part of his religion—for it is the son who performs all his last rites—over-rules all personal desire.

To the Indian woman also, who under Hindu law, cannot inherit, a son of her own or even of a co-wife, ensures the retention of her husband's land and wealth.

A Mahomedan widow can own and inherit property. This status—it would be well for Western reformers to note—was fixed long before the Western woman's own married woman's property act came into law.

The lot of the Hindu widow in India is unsatisfactory at best. Without a son, she is, practically, at the mercy of her husband's relations, near or distant, and is only entitled to her maintenance; and more often than not a mere pittance is considered sufficient for her needs.

In many instances, to keep the property intact, a wife, bearing no children, has herself insisted on the re-marriage of her husband. One distasteful instance, the writer remembers, was of a first wife who chose the second wife herself: a young girl, one-eyed and slightly crack-brained.

This second wife bore two children: but the elder retained—as was likely under the circumstances—all her power: and both the children were deeply attached to her, and she to them.

To a Maharani, an heir to the throne is almost a life and death question.

The heir of a co-wife counts as the son of all the Maharanis, the first wife counting as head-mother.

The allowing of an Indian queen, by the Government of India, to be regent during the minority of her son, has considerably ameliorated the lot of the Indian queen-widow.

Another point to be considered carefully is that the girl of the aristocratic class in India has no means of maintaining herself.

The mother instinct in all Asiatic girls is very strong; far stronger than that of her European sister. Unless, a tremendous change in social customs is effected first, there is no doubt that enforced monogamy will fall hardest on the very class it aims at protecting: that of the woman.

There is a far more delicate question, which must not be shirked.

There is, in India, a pampered class of men: a class that breeds strongest in hot countries. If this class, by law, is made to conform to monogamy, what will be the result? Merely a playing into the hands of the dancing girls and the courtesans.

A society entertainer told me that he once played for a certain Asiatic king on the occasion of a hair-cutting celebration of his sons.

When the curtain went up, the entertainer saw across

the footlights eighty youngsters, who appeared to his inexperienced eye, all of one age.

He was very curious to learn who these boys were and was stunned—a rather mild word—to learn they were all the sons of the king.

In olden days, no doubt, a collection of sons, grandsons, great-grandsons on a colossal scale made for the strength and prowess of a clan. In ancient history, one reads of a hundred sons as nothing unusual.

Could woman, on whom falls the greater burden, keep pace with amatory feats of this kind?

There is also the vexed question of divorce. The Mahomedan girl can be given " talak " (divorce). But in Hinduism, there is no divorce for husband or wife of the higher classes.

A dissatisfied man marries again, and his discarded wife remains in his house.

A woman, even if she has the privilege of divorce, is, in India, tarnished goods.

Her only possibility of happiness is to try and please her husband. It happens as often as not that the arrival of a second wife may be entirely the fault of the first wife.

Stranger, still, to Englishwomen, it is not unknown for a Princess of an Indian State, to ask her father-in-law to bring her, as a present, a " sister " : the designation of a co-wife. The writer, herself, heard this absurd request.

Four Ranis of a certain State commiserated, actually commiserated, with a certain Begum because she was the only wife.

" Oh! How dreadfully lonely you must be! " chorused the four Ranis: and one believes them sincere. So it is vain to try and solve this puzzle by applying to it the rules of another world. For if it is no longer true that East and West cannot meet; it is for ever true that the laws that are wise for the one are not necessarily wise for the other.

Each must be guided by what is expedient and necessary to the happiness of the majority of their kind.

CHAPTER IV

THE JAINS

THE Jains are one of the most influential and, possibly, one of the most misunderstood communities in India.

They sweep from West to East across Northern India : but have little power now down South where orthodox Brahminism, broken by Buddhism, reigns once more. It was Shri Shankaracharya, who swept away Jainism after its supercession of Buddhism.

The Jains are divided into two sects, the Swetambar and the Sthana-vasi, the principles of which are identical ; the difference, a wide one, being that of ritual.

It is to the Swetambar Jains that India owes its magnificent Jain-temples : the Palitana and Dilwara ones being world famous for their wonderful marble carving : real specimens of Jain architecture.

The Swetambar Jains are idol-worshippers : the Sthana-vasi Jains do not worship the idols ; though they keep the idols of their Tirthankars in temples and respect them.

There is a third sect " Digambars "—literally : naked ones. But the Jains no longer, look with favour on this third sect.[1] So far there is in existence to-day only one Digambar priest of note. He lives in a garden in Benares.

[1] Since this has been written there has been an agitation in favour of the revival of this sect.

The Digambars—as their name infers—wear no clothes.

The priests of the Swetambar sect wear two cloths: a loin-cloth and a shoulder-cloth.

The Sthana-vasi priest adds a small piece of canvas over his mouth, laced by loops of twisted tape over each ear.

Photographs of all sects of the priest-hood are very difficult to procure, because, strictly speaking, the taking of photographs is forbidden to the Jain monkhood.

But some devotee gets his own way where the most important priests are concerned: and these photographs, are available in limited numbers, and have a value that the mere layman will never appreciate unless he be of the Jain religion.[1]

The Jains have a monkhood, that is one of the most chaste in the world: that must never touch a woman, nor occupy the same carpet or mat as the opposite sex. Even the accidental touch of a baby girl means fasting for the monk for the whole day. This does not mean that the Jains do not respect women. On the contrary, the Jain religion—unlike Hinduism—allows women the use of the sacred "mantras," and initiates them into a nunnery more or less similar to the order of the monkhood.

The nuns are bound by their order, however, to respect the monks, and are not on terms of complete equality, holding a slightly subordinate position.

[1] In the All India Jain Conference of 1933, at Aimere, the film showing, among other scenes, the procession of the priests was an occasion of a good deal of dispute, and it was held up for a time by a certain section of Jains as contravening this law of prohibition. The chief objectors were, of course, the priests themselves; but it was pointed out to them that they not being a party to the act of filming, had contravened no law. Better feelings subsequently prevailing, the film is now being shown.

Monks and nuns alike walk barefooted: the former bareheaded.

They carry a whisk of soft wool to sweep away small insects in their way, and must not walk on grass. To ensure this rule being strictly observed, their religion forces them to spend four months of the rainy season in one place; whilst, at other times, they must not stay more than ten days in the same place.

Several reasons are given for this last rule; the preventing of worldly attachments, and of monks and nuns remaining a burden on a single set of people, being two of the most important. They beg their food twice a day in wooden bowls, and must not take more than they can eat at one meal. If, by oversight or want of judgment, they have received more than their needs, the unused food must be taken several miles out of the city and buried, lest it attract insect-life, and the monk or nun become a cause leading to its hurt or destruction.

They must always eat, sit, walk and guard every physical movement carefully for the same reason—lest they become responsible for the death of some sentient thing.

This scrupulous regard for animal and insect life has given rise to the wildest stories about the Jains.

One of the most absurd, generally believed by Europeans in India, is that the Jains pay beggars to sleep in blankets covered with bugs and fleas to ensure the insects a full meal.

This is an absolute libel: for blood food, of any description, is forbidden to the Jains by every ethic of their religion.

The monks and nuns are not allowed to travel in any

conveyance: though this rule dated from the days when trains and motors were not in existence, and no Jain monk could be a burden to man and beast.

Yet, strange paradox, to-day, whilst motors and trains are still strictly taboo, a sick monk or nun is allowed to be carried by men in a palanquin.

The same fear of destroying insect life makes the eating of roots one of the minor sins.

Every Jain town has a hermitage, called a "Pinjra-pol," where animals, birds and every form of insect life find sanctuary.

There is a separate building for insects of various sorts, almost hermetically closed.

The insects are placed inside through small apertures: and various grains are put in for their sustenance.

The building is opened out every twelve or fifteen years, inspected and cleaned.

Snakes and other poisonous reptiles are caught by a specially made clefted-stick; and there are men who are adepts at holding a snake in these sticks; snakes are not in the hermitage, but carried by these men to an uninhabited piece of jungle and left there.

It sounds a great deal of trouble and very absurd to the Western world: for to the people of this world it is so much easier to kill them. But it is just here that the spirit of sacrifice, so praised in Jain ethics, and cultivated so carefully, appears in its greatest form.

The writer knows, personally, of an instance where a Jain woman had a snake taken out of her house twice, before it returned the third time to bite her: and even though she died, the relatives took the snake out again, and left it in a far-away jungle.

It has been said that Jains are kinder to animals than men, instancing the palanquin carried by men in which sick priests travel: but it is forgotten that the will of the men who carry them can always be determined: if they grow tired they may demand rest; whilst an animal, under similar conditions, may be worked when unfit, weary or unwilling.

In these "pinjra-pols" old and worn-out animals are kept: animals suffering from diseases some—alas—incurable. The healthy ones go out for grazing in special fields: the latter are tended to, sometimes, one fears, not too satisfactorily, by veterinary surgeons; all are allowed to die a natural death.[1] Undoubtedly, at one time, these old hermitages were badly organised, and a good deal of money went to waste. It is more than possible that in many cases, a good deal of unnecessary suffering took place. But the evils have been greatly exaggerated: and the good done very much underestimated.

Many a hurt bird, many a frightened, lost creature of the woods, has been protected, restored to health, and returned to its old haunts: the writer can vouch for this personally.

The poor old horses are fed; some of them perhaps used; but only for processions: certainly not sold to take more work out of their tired, old bodies, as—to our discredit, be it said—the poor worn-out horses of England are sold. The Jain religion is essentially a religion of harmlessness, *ahimsa*; translated so badly, by the political

[1] In this connection, the writer has been instrumental in getting Jains and Hindus to found a new hospital, the Gurushri Shanti Vijayaji Hospital, Mt. Abu, which is run on up-to-date Western lines, retaining this Jain principle of not hastening death: pain, of course, alleviated by anæsthetics.

word non-violence; but harmlessness by word and thought as well as by deed.

If a monk or nun falls ill, he or she is allowed to remain in that place till recovery or death.

The death of a Jain monk is an event of sacred interest to a number of devout people, who come many miles to take a last look at the face of the dead priest: special merit is believed to be won by this act, particularly if the deceased priest was a man of some eminence or saintliness.

The priest's corpse is kept as long as twenty-four hours, an unusual time in India, to allow people from distant places to arrive in time. The body is placed in a sitting posture, kept in position by ropes, still in the white dress of the priesthood; sprinkled, now, with red powder: and in the case of the Sthana-vasi priests, for the first time, since initiation, without the white covering over the mouth. The corpse is placed in its old place amongst its pupils and brother-monks: and this seated monk, dead to all at last, is a sight of deep pathos—once seen, never to be forgotten.

Jain monks do not shave their beards, lips, or chins: but twice a year, they pluck the hair out. Some monks have terrible scars and sores due to this painful austerity.

The keynote of the Jain religion is sacrifice. Harmlessness, i.e., "Ahimsa" is placed at the head of the eight prime virtues that every Jain hopes, sometime or the other, to acquire in their fullness.

1. Harmlessness.
2. Subjection of all senses.
3. Kindness.
4. Patience.
5. Fullness of entire knowledge.

6. Truth.
7. Fixedness in penance.
8. Knowledge, void of doubt.

The monks of both sects are divided into teachers and ascetics.

Vocation makes the one or the other.

The teachers preach in public places set apart for the purpose, and however busy a Jain may be, it is part of his religious duty to attend these sermons in person, with, if possible, all the members of his family.

Pilgrimages on holy days, the birthdays of "Tirthankers" are great occasions especially among the Swetambar sect. Large bands of pilgrims are formed: and the devout walk some hundreds of miles with bands of monks and nuns. There is all the paraphernalia of a regular caravan including a temple on wheels.

More often than not, the cost of the excursion is entirely defrayed by some devout merchant, who is the leader of the expedition: (Sangh)—that collects more and more Jains "en route" to the place of pilgrimage.

The bigger "sanghs" cost anything from over fifty thousand to over a lakh of rupees.

The Jains who are a sect distinctly apart from the Hindus have, strangely enough, all their ceremonies performed by Brahmins.

There are many reasons advanced for this complexity: but the principle one is probably because the Jain priests, vowed to non-interference in any worldly concern, cannot officiate in marriage ceremonies: or, in fact, any ritual requiring daily attendance. As regards the cooks also: the Jains have intensely conservative views about food: and they keep Brahmins to do their cooking in preference even to members of their own sect, though they eat food cooked by the ladies of their family.

The Jains are married at an early age: and the Jain ladies are usually splendid house-wives and cooks: still excelling in those arts of butter-making, the making of pickles, preserves, healing ointments and cooling decoctions, reminiscent of one's great-grandmother's times, when women had the leisure and inclination for these gentle arts.

Present-day agitation is touching the modern Jain lady in many respects to her grave detriment; but this type is happily still in the minority.

Water because it is filled with organic life is used sparingly by most Jains.

Strangely enough, however, it is used freely in the houses of the Swetambar sect: because bathing is a rite necessary to the worship of idols. But the water used must first be boiled.

There seems to be a jumble of ethics here, for it appears from enquiry that the boiling of the water makes the user less, personally, responsible for the loss of organic life involved.

The other sect uses water in very limited quantities: even to the point of unpleasantness, sometimes.

The Jains are lavish in their hospitality.

They work hard, drive tremendous bargains: but disgorge a good deal of their inordinate profits in charity; though, very often, one suspects them still of having their eyes on the main chance, i.e., some profit in a future life: for your true Jain believes, with all his heart, that his charities, in this world, determine the amount of money he will have at his disposal in the next.

But it is quite enough to his credit, nowadays, that he believes in charity or a next world at all.

The Jains are thrifty and hard-working.

Usury and politics have forced their way into business helping to its deterioration; but the majority still retain qualities that will make the loss of their community—as a community—a sad thing for India.

CHAPTER V

FAKIRS AND SADHUS[1]

THE Fakirs and Sadhus of India have always exercised tremendous influence, capturing the imagination not only of a great number of the population of India, but of the people of countries, outside India. Superstitious fear of the abnormal is, no doubt, the root cause of this reverence of the masses : but not so where practical men—worldly, even cynical men—men with only shreds of faith in things religious, are concerned : nor could it be the cause of the interest of the philosopher or the man of religion.

Is it real holiness that holds the human mind, that sways the heart, and gains for the Sadhu devotion, reverence or admiration ? Or is it merely the hunger of the human soul for something to worship ?

Some of the holiest men in the world are indeed "sadhus," fakirs and ascetics : but in India, as elsewhere, their value as an order is daily counting for little or nothing.

Yet, perhaps, this is too sweeping a statement : for, after all, only a little leaven is required to raise the whole.

Yet,—one cannot emphasize this too strongly, especially

[1] A young man brother of a "Sadhu" whose name is a household word in India, wrote rather indignantly about any exposure of "Sadhus." But later, helped to reason by his great brother, he saw that the biggest enemies of the good "Sadhus" are indeed these impostors who assume, so lightly, the sacred garb.

(Note : A Fakir is a Mahomedan term : a Sadhu, a Jain or Hindu term).

where women are concerned,—the dangers attendant on this subservience of mind to " Sadhus " are great.

Many of these so-called " Sadhus " keep their unfortunate pupils in a state bordering on the hypnotic, where the weakening of judgment, loss of physical health and morals are all but a question of time.

There are some women whose sense of moral proportion has been completely altered by these so-called " Gurus," and mind, wealth and body alike have been placed at their feet; for it is generally believed by a large section of the Indian public that this is the easiest way of all to secure the supernatural powers of the " Guru."

It is not the province of a book like this to define a Guru: nor restate the old truism that there are no short cuts to the religious life: the one straight road being for all time the road of clean and perfect morality.

To advise the avoidance of wandering " Sadhus "; the subjecting to a careful scrutiny even those for whom decent people vouch for; the eschewing of any " Sadhu " whose influence tends to the lowering of a single ideal, would savour of impertinence; and yet so dangerously do these inferior " Sadhus " make use of the art of hypnotism that the writer who has many friends amongst the best " Sadhus " feels bound to do so, and no single one of these good " Sadhus " will object to this advice.

The writer has written elsewhere of Jain Sadhus. The stern restrictions laid on them preventing all contact with the opposite sex, help to keep this order chaste: though there has, of late, been a tendency to the relaxing of these restrictions. This, in itself, is not a thing to be regretful about; for restrictions may hamper virtue, and cannot prevent vice, if vice be inherent. Women partly, perhaps, on account of their weaker, more confiding nature, partly because it is incumbent on them to hear religious discourses, are, by far, the biggest proportion of a " Sadhu's " followers : to them, again, is due the lamentable amount of bazaar gossip that comes into the " upashryas " (hermitages) where part of the time, once spent wholly in listening to the deeds of Ramchandra, or Vikramaditya, or the great Tirthankars, goes to the relating of quarrels, bad investments and the good and ill deeds—mostly the latter—of neighbours.

The " Sadhus " who listen, forget their rôle of indifference to all things worldly, assuming the modern rôles of barristers, pleaders and judges.

This has brought about a loss of prestige, especially amongst Jain Sadhus, and many a " Sadhu " has but exchanged his dress, being to all intents and purposes still a house-holder at heart.

There are other men, strong, sturdy of no sect ; beggars, pure and simple, who also call themselves " Sadhus." There are they who are opium eaters ; some harmless, some not so harmless.

There are smokers of hemp (ganja), and those who practise revolting austerities.

The yellow robe in India once sign of greatness, hides many a dangerous character : for in this country of the simple and good, the dress alone is sufficient protection against all enquiry.

Intriguers, criminals wanted by the police, find no better disguise than ashes daubed over face and body, saffron marks and red ochre smeared across forehead.

A notorious dacoit wanted by the police of several States and afterwards caught, confessed to the experience of seeing, once, the very Jemadar of the posse who caught him, prostrating meekly before him on Girnar, the famous place of pilgrimage in Junagadh, where, the dacoit daubed with ashes, devoutly counting his beads, had gained a much needed respite and rest. This quasi-sadhu is now languishing in an Agency prison, the Agency having a bigger crime sheet against him; but there are some of his kind not so safely interned.

The questions again arise: are there no good Sadhus left in India? Have they, no longer, the power which was but lately trumpeted forth as pertaining alone to India and her Mahatmas?

Once more the writer reiterates: there are good and noble Sadhus still; gentle, loving, harmless and pure; and by the beauty of their simple lives alone, at once an inspiration and guide to the sincere.

It is questionable, however, whether they are better teachers than those that every religion has already given to man, except where mankind would appear not to have yet learnt the truths, enunciated by these great ones.

The letters of life have to be relearnt over and over again.

There are Sadhus who sit in solitary caves, including in their personal salvation that of the universes.

They are not selfish as the writer once thought.

They see no separation between the part and the whole: the small atom rising within the great, cannot but uplift the whole.

In their meditation, they pray with every force at their command, with the accumulated power engendered by their austerity and will, for the upliftment of the earth and the relief of pain, showering the world with a blessing so magnetic as to be felt if one be near. Purified thought is the most powerful of all the gifts of God to man.

It may well be because of these great " Sadhus " that the other types are tolerated: even as nature burdens herself with thousands of useless seeds, for the sake of the few that germinate.

Have Sadhus and Fakirs super-natural powers?

Has the writer ever met one who has these powers: the powers that romanticists have written of, and the world has sought for and still seeks with unabated energy?

CHAPTER VI

THE SADHUS (*continued*)

IT is rather difficult in a work of this kind to drag in metaphysics; yet before one deals with a few of the many religions of India it would be misleading not to give a summary of the philosophy that has made India great. The writer who has studied this philosophy has summed it up for her own satisfaction thus:

1. The positing of one GREAT ENERGY that can with-withdraw everything into ITSELF even as the sleeper draws into his brain cells when he sleeps all that is *his* conception.
2. The positing of a Creator that creates, by the infusion of DIVINE ENERGY: and in turn links up his creation with Himself.
3. The positing of a creation that in man becomes conscious of that ENERGY and would use it for the specializing (uplifting or degrading) of forms.
4. The creation of a veil of ignorance, which when forms are degraded hides from man his real power. (The degraded forms are worn away by time.)
5. The creation of a definite set of laws: making upliftment of a form to bring happiness and degradation pain.

The seeds of degradation are burnt by yoga,[1] or allowed to ripen in future births (finally destroyed by Time.)

6. Positing this energy of force as unceasing.

This energy can be sent through a human dynamo—the Messiahs of the world—carefully prepared; isolated from the world. They alone—the Gurus—can regulate it to lower needs, supplying by mere contact (the same ideals making the necessary affinity) deficiencies in man. This soul-force has no affinity with worldly matter or matters.

It is a spiritual light: a pulsating flame, with nothing imaginative about it: a tangible thing that can be seen with the human eye and felt as heat. Only those who have this divine force are Mahatmas. This force, this power, so sought after by ascetics and laymen alike, is one of the rarest and most secret things in the universe: and its acquisition is dependent upon nothing less than affinity to divinity, by cultivating divine virtues.

The writer knows of only two persons in India who have that force: and both bear unknown names, despite the tremendous power they wield.

From these great ones to the ones on view is saddening: comment however is superfluous: one may confine oneself to facts alone, and leave the rest to the reader's judgment.

During the last Kumbhamela, the *Times of India* had a head-line: "Five thousand Vairagis run amuck at Hardwar."

The papers went on to relate that five thousand of these "vairagis" put up a free fight in the Kumbhamela

[1] See the Author's *Philosophy of Yoga*"—Messrs. Luzac and Co., London.

because they were disappointed about the distribution of food.

Now the term " Vairagi " is a Sanscrit word : it means devoid of passion, devoid of desire (raga). Our true Vairagi must court perpetual poverty and chastity. They must subsist entirely upon alms, and these must be given willingly.

The Vairagis have no definite form of worship : but they are considered to be devotees of Ram and Vishnu. Some of them live in monasteries and take pupils : but a number of them are without fixed abode.

There is another class of " Sadhu," the Sanyasis, called Tridandies (literally—three sticks). The Tridandi Sanyasis carry always three sticks with them wherever they go : emblems of their control over speech, body and mind. They are mostly Brahmins, and have passed through the stages of student life, and that of the house-holder. They are strictly forbidden to touch any metal or fire : and their drinking vessels are made from gourds. Their food is begged from the houses of the Brahmins of the Vaishnava faith. They are, principally, followers of the reformer Ramanuja.

The Nagar ascetics resemble both the Vairagis and Sanyasis : but, as their names signify, they wear no clothes at all on their bodies. They are consequently not held in very high repute.

Strangely enough, though they also are forbidden to touch metals or fire, they carry with them firearms and swords.

The Dandi Sanyasis carry a single staff with several knots tied with a piece of cloth dyed in red ochre at the top.

It is believed that this cloth covers their sacred thread.

They can never be without this staff: and even whilst sleeping, they are not supposed to allow the staff to leave the hand.

The Dandi Sanyasis shave their hair and beards, wear a single loin cloth, and eat only one meal a day which they beg from the houses of Brahmins alone.

The majority of them worship Shri Shankaracharya as the incarnation of Shiva: and some of them wear the Shiva mark in ashes on the forehead.

This mark is supposed to represent the two-petalled mind-lotus[1] of yoga, but the original thought is now almost lost: for it has degenerated to-day, even to three transverse lines. Others worship Niranjan: a deity without attributes. They dispose of their dead, by floating them down some sacred stream or river; if this is not possible; by burying them, an unusual procedure in a land where cremation is the usual method of disposal.

The Dandies believe that the bodies of "Sadhus," purified by asceticism, hold as long as the least atom remains the magnetism of Divine Power, and, therefore, consider the bodies of their order holy enough to raise, by this magnetism, the vibrations of anyone who comes near to these remains. The idols of certain temples, are supposed to have the same magnetic power imparted to them either by holding the magnetic power of some great soul, or of the sacred mantras, and no idol is ever worshipped before a certain power has been placed in it by appropriate ceremonies. It seems likely that in the

[1] Ajna lotus.

present iron age, this power has been lost; for it is now believed that the building of a temple to-day brings bad luck.

The Dandies are initiated in a strange manner: the inner part of the knee is cut, blood squeezed out, and offered to the god Bhairava.

This certainly looks like a survival of some old human blood-sacrifice.

The Yogis,[1] of whom the Western world has heard so much, are followers of several schools of philosophy, that of Patanjala and Kanada being amongst the most well-known. The word Yogi comes from a Sanscrit root meaning to join.

The Jivatma, soul in the form of man, has for its aim the "rejoining" (Yuj) of itself to the Paramatma, the universal soul.

To achieve this great end, several schools have evolved processes all of which have had their vogue: the controlling of the breath in the body, believing the breath to be a link between man's own energy and the energy of the over-soul: "pranayama," is one of the processes well known to the world of to-day.

Continued practice in "pranayama" brings about the suppression of breath at will: and with this control over breath, the yogi undoubtedly achieves certain powers over the elements and the laws of gravity alike, and is able to perform what by virtue of being abnormal are called miracles.

When by any method, the identification with this over-

[1] Note that a yogi-proper has no home, no division, no sect and no order, because the universe is his home; he sees no differences anywhere. The name is used here conveniently to describe the various schools of Yoga, followed by various ascetics.

soul is complete, the yogi takes no more human forms except of his own free will.

These ascetics in Yoga are divided into sects: each sect identifying itself with its founder and worshipping that founder as the incarnation of Shiva Himself.

Goraknath founded the sect of "Yogis" called Kanphatas (literally—bored ears). The Kanphatas bore their ears, and insert rings in them at the time of their initiation. They mark their foreheads and smear their bodies with ashes, and they are sometimes dressed in a small loin cloth, at other times in garments dyed with red ochre.

The Paramhansas (great swans) dress in sackcloth. Their order requires them to beg their food and live in caves.

The "Aghories" are the most feared of all the Indian ascetics. The writer met one in Mount Abu, with matted locks piled high on his head: staring-eyes, red and burning, and nails at least seven inches long. He leaned on a cleft-stick in the attitude of a crouching animal: and it is not unlikely that he assumed that position for the benefit of his followers. For your true "Aghori" according to popular superstition, takes the form of a wild animal—preferably the panther or tiger—at will. The writer was assured, in all sincerity, that an "Aghori" of Mount Abu annoyed by a man who would persist, out of curiosity, in following him to his cave after sunset, repeatedly warned him that at night the ascetic's form would change, and with the change, all human mercy would disappear.

The follower through fear desisted for awhile, but once again, partly through greed for some favour, partly curiosity, the man went to the cave of the Aghori, and from that day up to the day of writing nothing more has been heard of him.

His friends and relations searched in vain, and sincerely believe that he has really been eaten by this Aghori.

The Aghoris are obliged, by the rules of their order to eat anything and everything put in their begging bowl, even excrement. The writer knows of a case where a profane person actually tested this last and found the Aghori obeyed the rule.

They smear their bodies with filth and carry it about with them, sometimes in a skull and sometimes in a wooden pot.

Despite the fear they inspire, they still have a following : for they are supposed, above all ascetics, to have unusual and great powers : the greatest of which is the alleged possession of the philosopher's stone.

In this instance, the late Nawab Sahib of Palanpur used to relate a very strange tale. One day, he and his companions walking about the hills of Mount Abu found themselves completely lost. Night began to fall and in those old days, the jungles abounded in tigers and panthers. Despair fell upon the party, when suddenly, as if from the rock itself, a wild figure with matted hair emerged. He bade them not to fear, but follow him to his cave. He fed them, and was exceptionally pleased with the late Nawab Sahib who was a deeply religious man, and devoted to Sadhus.

After some talk he called the Nawab Sahib aside and scraping away some ashes in his cave brought to view two large bars of gold : "Bid your followers lift them up, and take them away. They are yours. I shall then show you the way back to the main road," said the ascetic.

The Nawab Sahib, fully aware that this ascetic had the philosoper's stone refused, and begged him instead to give him that.

The Sadhu sighed. He bade them sleep for the present.

So the party slept in the cave, waking on the morrow to find themselves miles away from ascetic or cave. The Nawab Sahib tried in vain to locate the place, but from that day onwards, neither ascetic nor cave was ever again seen by the Nawab.

Most tourists to Benares have seen the " Sky-faced ascetics (Akash Mukhi). These ascetics continue looking at the sky till the muscles of their necks get fixed in that position. They wear yellow garments, allow their hair to grow, and their pupils daily smear their bodies with ashes, collect alms from the devout and curious, and pass their lives in this strange way.

The Nakhi-ascetics allow their nails to grow through their hands.

The Uddharbahus have a somewhat similar austerity: keeping a hand in an extended position, till all the muscles stiffen.

Other ascetics have stranger austerities.

They never walk, but roll from village to village, town to town, fed by the gentler Indians.

Others, again, vow never to rest or sleep in the normal way.

The writer saw one in a reclining posture, resting by means of a plank and ropes slung over a tree, with legs that were swollen to about six times their normal size.

His condition was, indeed, pitiable, and his moans attracted much sympathy.

The writer tried to discover why he thought this peculiar form of asceticism necessary for his salvation, but could receive no lucid answer.

Sometimes these extraordinary austerities are meant to be expiation of a heinous crime, but more possibly the desire for the power referred to in the beginning of the chapter leads a man on, till nature creates a mania or deformity, which passes beyond the ascetic's control.

CHAPTER VII

Religions and Fairs

WHEN ascetics are divided into so many sects, it is not to be wondered that the religions of India are many, its people divided and sub-divided into various castes of thought.

India, with all its caste differences settled, would still be split by sectarianism; for it is a country where every year sees the rise of a new cult, raised to eminence by the devotion or credulity of a simple people. These cults hold chiefly by the emotions, and their followers are elevated or degraded according to the height or depth of the particular emotion evoked.

Sometimes love plays its part: at another time, fear. One cannot judge off hand as to the worthlessness of certain strange, even repellent symbols or rituals; for many a lost thread to ancient esotericism can often be found again, tangled and broken, running through the old rituals of old-time faiths.

The Vamacharis (left-hand worshippers)[1] of Shiva and Shakti are prevalent in certain States. These exoteric worshippers have done more to bring the Tantras into disrepute than any other sect in India to-day. Men and women would flock to the temples at night for the so-called kaula-circle, where priests would sprinkle the assembly

[1] See the Author's *Tantrik Doctrine of Immaculate Conception.*

in couples—male and female—with sacred water. To be correct, this sprinkling should be haphazard, but the writer heard from the lips of a one-time follower, of this sect, himself, that the priest was often bribed to sprinkle certain couples together. These couples retired to a private chamber where the man was supposed to have worshipped the woman as " mother."

But many great scandals arose : and this form of worship is held in considerable disrepute. One of the priests of the sect, now a sanyasin, told the writer that he had vowed to break up every kaula-circle in India.

In this connection the writer had a letter, from the head of an occult society in answer to an enquiry of hers ; it is not without interest : " a genuine Shri Vidya Upasaka," writes the learned man, " must always have his lady, or her lord with him or her. Only the *really initiated* (all italics his own) know the use of the other sex in these practices, which while on the border-land of sex, are actually entirely devotional, mystic and *supremely holy*. The *least* trace of evil or sensual, sexual desire would turn the Sadhaka into a beast : in fact amongst Sadhakas there are many who prowl about and hide their sensualism in the maze of rituals and ' poojas.' "

The worship of Radhaji, the beloved of Krishna, is another worship of the feminine principle : but its ritual is pure, and the devotees follow the rules laid down by the strictest of Vaishnavas.

In Dwarka, there is still a certain amount of temple rivalry between the devotees of Lakshmi, the wife of Krishna, and Radha, his beloved.

There are different temples dedicated to Krishna ; one where the " blue god "—the god of dispassion—stays with Lakshmi, and one where he stays with Radha. Exactly how Radhaji came to be associated with Krishna, is a problem still puzzling the heads of Indian Pundits to-day. The Shrimad Bhagvad, which gives a detailed account of Krishna's youthful life, makes no mention of her at all.

The Radha Vallabhis have a special hermitage (math) at Brindaban, where the watchmen call the hour of the night thus: "Ra—dhe—Krishna"; and Radha's name is still the one that is associated most with that of Krishna.

Certain Sadhus, called Sakhi-Bavas, go about in feminine attire, personating Radha, and worship Krishna thus attired.

They hope, ingeniously, to win Krishna's favour quicker by this method, believing that He will be more attracted by a worship from one in the form of His beloved. These "Sadhus" wear jewels and dance before the idol. They are still to be seen in Jeypore, but their numbers are yearly lessening; and they do not command the respect of the public that they did formerly.

The Nimavat sect of the Vaishnava faith, chiefly found in Bengal, are also worshippers of Radha-Krishna: but the sect is a completely different one from that in the West of India.

The caste mark of this Bengal sect is black whilst the one in Western India is red; black being considered inauspicious.

A sect found all over Kathiawar, is that of the Swami Narayan Sampradaya, founded by Sayjanand Swami. This sect worships Nur Narayan, the sun and moon, as well as Radha-Krishna. The rules are very strict as regards vegetarian food, cleanliness in eating, and the eating from the hands of no other than a member of its own sect.

The principal festivals are Vasant Panchmi (the month of Maha) the fifth day of the dark half, and Gokal Ashtami (the month of Shravan) the eighth day of the dark half when their teachers sprinkle members with coloured paint on the first mentioned day, and the whole sect—with every devout Hindu—fasts on the second day till midnight.

Gokal Ashtami is the birthday of Krishna, and all Hindu India fasts, or at the most eats " falahar " (literally—fruit-food, but nuts and roots are now included). Though it is a day of fasting, it is still a day of festivity, and the finest clothes in honour of the great event are worn.

Agriculturists in pure white, wearing their large gala turbans, men with roughened clumsy hands, and eyes faded with long staring at sun-lit fields, or youthful and strong: Rajputs in velvet or gold; shepherds, tall and gnarled; long-haired " Kolis " with bold eyes and red turbans, fantastically dressed; " Khavases " apeing the Rajput dress; the Dheds—an untouchable caste—apart, but very independent and gay; all crowd through the streets in festive attire, some to the fairs that are always held that day, some to the temples. Their women are even more gaily dressed than their men folk. The wives of the agriculturists dress very like women of the zenana. They wear simple bodices, a flared skirt and a sari, and their faces are covered because of their gentle birth.

The shepherdesses wear ivory bangles reaching up to their elbows, while their head-dress flows loose from their proud heads. They are the happiest of all this day, for it is their special privilege on Gokal Ashtami to go to the palace and sing the " Rasada " : the " circle-dance " that Krishna danced with the shepherdesses of old in Brindaban centuries ago. Those old shepherdesses could not have danced and sung with more loving zest and fervour than these of to-day: their powerful voices ring startlingly loud above the drums, and the clash and the clink of their bangles lend a wildness to the scene.

They are big, tall women, stooping low down to each other's ankles, rising and swinging round in wide circles, again touching hands, now low, now high, with convulsive jerks of their well built bodies. These simple primitive people of the India that is India are completely untouched by the propaganda of the agitator. They have few wants and are extremely happy. The poverty of the Western world is not here in the States. One sees this definitely at the fairs: few or no women are without jewellery, silver or gold.

It is at these fairs the people buy the annual clothes for the family, and toys for their little children: coloured combs from Bombay; paper-weights from Ahmedabad; stiffened loin cloths; hideous photographs of Gokal Ram as a badly proportioned baby, all head and little body; treasures all guaranteed to catch the eye of a simple folk, though the wiser of them will have none of these fancy things.

Wandering Brahmin boys with bright red caste marks on their forehead, and yellow sandal spots over their eyes hold out trays of red powder and rice, and in return for alms make the red "chanla," the auspicious mark on the forehead: the mark of Lakshmi, the goddess of fortune, with a grain or two of rice pressed on it afterwards, with the coveted Brahmin blessing. At midnight everyone crowds to the Vaishanava temples, and exactly on the stroke of twelve the bells ring and the priests re-announce the birth of Gokalji.

Everyone rushes in the temple to do the " darshana " of the newly-born baby. The fast is over.

The largest temples of the Swami Narayan sect are at Vadtal and Sapaya, where there are images of Radha-Krishna, Surya Narayan and Swami Sayjanand, with sometimes the monkey-god Hanumanji. Sapaya being the birthplace of Swami Sayjanand is accorded a special sanctity by his followers, and pilgrims from all over the country flock to it on the Gokal Ashtami day.

The Vallabhacharis, followers of Vallabha, have a different cult. Vallabha was not a recluse: so not only is it incumbent on his followers to be family men; but the heads of the temples are not allowed to be celibates either.

These men are called " Gosains " and their followers are enjoined by the scriptures to worship the priests with body, mind and wealth to gain salvation.

The power of this sect was, at one time, almost unlimited, and, though still powerful, the age does not look with pleasure at the excesses that come automatically when religion makes sacred unrestrained gifts of body and mind.[1]

The followers of the Gosains worship Krishna in his child-form, and the idol is dressed and tended with all care.

There are eight distinct ceremonies during the day: the idol is washed and dressed, placed upon a throne, and food is presented to it, whilst the favoured few wait without.

[1] The head of this sect both in Oodaipur and Bombay has recently been disinherited because of his marriage with a dancing girl. Criticism of any sort would have been impossible fifty years ago.

When the slight meal is over, the idol is anointed with "atta"—scent—and attired in splendid robes of gold-brocade, a different colour for each day, when the worshippers are allowed to enter and have "Darshana" (literally—sight) of the idol.

At midday, a grand feast is placed before the idol in gold or silver vessels and its worshippers partake of this afterwards,—not, of course, in the temple vessels—after which the god goes to sleep till afternoon.

His worshippers wake him up for the evening meal; when the idol is again washed, freshly perfumed and re-attired for the evening "darshan." At night the idol is placed upon a gold or silver swinging couch with all the appurtenances necessary for the night near him, and the votaries lock up the Temple and retire for the night.

A number of women of this sect dance annually at Brindaban in commemoration of Krishna's dance with the shepherdesses.

The writer was told by a Shāstri, that some of them dance till a kind of hysteria sets in; though they fall down with fatigue they rise again, and go on dancing till completely exhausted. In many cases death has even occurred. The most celebrated of the Gosain temples is that of Shri Nath Dwar in Ajmer.

The Raavats, whose founder was Ramanand, are worshippers of the God Vishnu in His Ram incarnation. Rama and Sita are worshipped, together, in the form of the black saligram stone and the Tulsi-balsam plant, which are venerated as emblems of Ram and Sita. The Ramavats like nearly every other sect are also split up into sects too numerous to mention in detail.

The writer could detail still further of other sects, but this diversity in the religious life is not confined to the East alone, and except for the intrinsic interest to the Western world of these religious sects of India, there is no point in dwelling on these strange differences.

CHAPTER VIII

Customs and Beliefs

IN India there are many customs based on Holy Writ: many that hold little of religious significance, and far many more that have absolutely no claim to the attention they receive other than that of popular usage. These last customs are designated: "Dosi Shastra" (the writ of the old women) and strangely enough, not only is their hold on popular imagination strong, but they are followed often to the detriment of the race.

The beating of breasts; tearing out of hair; the heart-rending shrieks of mourners, real and professional alike, continuing throughout the conventional period of mourning are of this kind.

From the day of bereavement, the friends and acquaintances, rich and poor alike, are obliged to make condolence visits: the men with white turbans,—for white and black are both mourning colours in India,—covered with a white cloth, which they lower over their faces; the women, like so many ghosts, their saris covering their faces, all beat their breasts, and cry at the top of their voices.

This continues from morning till night without intermission. As one band of mourners goes, another band comes, and each endeavours to out-rival the other. Professional "miranis" (singers) arrive when a great person dies to sing doleful songs, dancing round in a circle as they sing.

Their voices are extremely cheerful, marriages and funerals alike mean money for the singers. The theme in bereavements is necessarily sad, and the drum, sign of auspiciousness, is absent; but the sound of the drum is more than made up by the slap of the hands on the breasts of the singers. The beat of bare feet also sound, marking time to this doleful human drum.

Only those who have seen this dreadful travesty of mourning, with the real mourners strung up to so great a pitch of hysteria, that the streets resound with their piercing cries, can form an estimate of the dreadful consequences this custom sows in social life.

Several permanent bad cases of hysteria have developed from a day of mourning.

The writer knows of certain maid-servants sent on a condolence visit to a neighbouring State who beat their breasts so severely as to injure permanently some of the nerves; and another maid-servant who was asthmatic from that day.

At least two Indian States in Kathiawar have now placed a ban on this barbarous custom, the first being Limbdi, whose ruler, Sir Daulat Sinhji, shares with the ruler of Baroda the honour of being the foremost reformer in India.

A certain prince once told the writer that going through the streets of an Indian town one day, he found the road blocked by a number of women-mourners of the better class. Their hair had fallen down, the head-covering also, and their breasts were bare, whilst a crowd, with the vagabond element prevailing, stood around, actually laughing and enjoying the fun.

From the moment of bereavement till the end of a complete year no opportunity is given for the healing hand of time to cure the wound : it is kept deliberately open by this custom of having professional mourners. This professional mourning is counted as an honour to the dead.

Another Hindu custom, injurious to the health of the very young, is the "Avrat" vow which terminates on the day preceding the first day of the new moon of the month of Ashad—August.

This vow is part of a miscellaneous collection of vows, all of which have, for their object, the gaining of some worldly benefit.

The "Avrat" vow, which obliges a young unmarried Indian girl during five consecutive years from the 11th to the 15th day of the dark half of the month of Ashad, to keep awake the whole of the 14th night till the 15th evening, is for the long life of a future husband. The writer has seen the vow kept religiously by ladies of the zenana who have a whole troop of maid-servants to sing, dance and play with them the whole night. The piteous condition of the girls towards the 15th evening, as with reddened eyes they are driven—in the case of zenana girls—to the lake where their little offerings,—pots of sowed wheat and barley and a clay image of the goddess,—are immersed, must be seen to be realised.

Many of these girls are of tender age and they, too, reap unhappy consequences ; some are seriously ill for days afterwards ; but the awful fear engendered by the superstition that a girl who does not do the "Avrat" becomes a widow, is too irretrievable a disaster not to want to avoid it, at any cost.

The pathos of it all lies in the fact that several girls

who, with fullest faith, have religiously kept the "Avrat" vow have yet become widows.

Certain fasts can be ameliorated by eating "phal-ahar" (corrupted in Kathiawar into "faral"). A whole list of allowed eatables comes under this heading: potatoes, roots of every kind, ladies'-fingers, spinach and a certain kind of rice, though the original word means fruit alone.

There is another strange custom which requires of most Indian girls the complete shaving of her head at least once in youth. The writ of the old women insists on this as essential, especially after chickenpox: for, it says, if this is not done lightning may fall on the girl, or her eyes suffer in old age.

Many a fine head of hair has been sacrificed to this tradition: the writer saw the injury done to two heads of hair.

Another custom, which is dangerous in the extreme—because of the infection it spreads—is that of taking smallpox patients after ten days to the shrine of the goddess Shital: the scabs are left there as a votive-offering.

No thought of germs, or the infection left there, deters these people from the committance of this act: the Indian masses care naught for germs. The careless way they spit about the place; their nose-blowing, displaying a callousness to themselves and to others, has to be seen to be believed.

At several boys' schools, there is an allotted time for the blowing of noses, and every boy in the school leaves his class, blows his nose between finger and thumb,—violently or temperately, anywhere,—and every finger and thumb, then, wipes itself automatically on the nearest wall or post.

The headmaster of one of these schools told the writer

in all seriousness, that finding the continual nose-blowing of his pupils made havoc in the time of lessons, he had deputed his assistants to fix a special time, when the whole school *en masse* could do it once for all. There was no thought of discarding the action altogether.

The writer once saw the platform of a station[1] before a Prince's saloon thoroughly swept and cleaned, and a few minutes afterwards a band of young men pass by who without any consideration, whatsoever, spewed streams of betel juice from out of their mouths on to the freshly cleaned platform.

Another inconsiderate custom is the sprinkling of paint and coloured water during the famous "Holi" festival on every passer-by.

Where the mere sprinkling of coloured water is concerned, the festival is fairly harmless, possibly beneficient.

A prince once told the writer it was the only way to get a section of the people to wash itself and its clothes—but the ruining of the clothes of another by strong dyes, the abuse hurled at everyone make this festival not unlike that of the Roman Saturnalia. It is permissible for the "loafer-class," for whom the writer's princely friend assures her the Holi was primarily intended, to shower abuse on each and every one at Holi time.

The filthiest language is used and it is treated as part of the day's amusement: respectable women are obliged to remain in their houses for, at least, the three principal days of the Holi.

Certain wise princes are now passing emergency laws to deal with the nuisance.

[1] Rajkot.

CUSTOMS AND BELIEFS

One quaint and pleasant Indian custom, which claims some religious authority, is the placing of pen, ink and paper, and coloured rice in pretty patterns, to entice the Goddess of Luck—Vidhata—to write the good-fortune of the newly-born baby.

The ceremony proper takes place on the sixth day after the child is born. A Brahmin-priest recites the necessary incantations, and the child is left alone in the room for a few minutes with the coloured rice, the pen and the paper.

The paper remains always blank, the pen and ink appear unused, but it is firmly believed that Vidhata has done her duty, and the destiny of the child has been carefully and properly recorded.

The propitiation of the many gods and goddesses is a great business in the lives of these simple Indian people.

It has been suggested that those Indians who have had educational facilities, have now no time in their busier lives for the comparative ' frills ' of picturesque tradition. But the writer can vouch that these customs still prevail in the houses of the great and the educated, as well as in those of the poor and the ignorant.

The slow dance round a small brazier of charcoal fire at sunset for nine days preceding Dasserah, and on the night of the Dasserah, chanting certain songs, is a well-known method of propitiating the goddess.

It is also believed that during these ten days, she rides in her chariot through the sky; and woe betide the unlucky wight who, during these days, sleeps in the open, or under a tree!

The writer knows of a maid-servant, in a certain palace in Kathiawar, who has one leg several inches shorter than the other, because,—she assures everyone, and certainly believes it herself,—she slept during the Dasserah days, under a tree, and the Goddess' chariot went over her leg.

At weddings, the Hindu bride and bridegroom have to walk round the sacred fire three times, the woman's sari tied to the man's neck-cloth.

Amongst the poorer classes, the first of the bridal pair to sit down after these circumambulations is destined by fate to be the virtual ruler of the house: so it is believed.

Neither the bride nor bridegroom, in a becoming state of modesty, can at this time make any personal attempt to decide this for themselves, but the friends and relatives of bride and bridegroom do try to help the fates by pulling their respective clients to the seat first.

It is very serious, and very funny to watch.

Another custom is the curious one of advertising the forthcoming advent of a first child by sending out invitations to friends to be present at a seventh month ceremony called " Agani " (fire).

The religious prayers recited on this occasion have spiritual authority; but not the additions of suggestive songs and the brother-in-law's slap, with a hand covered with red powder to make a red mark, on the cheek of his sister-in-law.

The expectant mother heavily draped, supported by her girl friends, walks to the place where the " pooja " is to be done, and from her bed-room to the place of worship, an unmarried girl goes before her and places a betel nut and a piece of money under each foot of the expectant mother over which she treads. This money and the betel nuts go to the girl afterwards and are specially prized as auspicious.

Nails must be collected and thrown in water: hair

must not be burnt or the owner's head will nod in old age: a married woman must not wash her hair on Tuesday, because it brings danger to the husband; nor on Wednesday, for then the brothers suffer. One who returns from a journey must see on his return something auspicious, and as the most auspicious sight is that of a virgin (or a married woman) with a full waterpot on her head, this is ensured by keeping a bevy of ladies with water-pots on their heads ready to meet relative or guest before the house is entered. These women with water-pots always meet Princes and great people.

An Indian child does not get its name in the same haphazard manner of the child of the West.

The hour and minute of the Indian child's birth are very carefully noted: the family priest waits outside the confinement chamber of rich and poor alike; and it is he who looks up the syllables to start a name which will prove auspicious to a child born at that particular time, and no Hindu parent would dream of giving a name not beginning with the syllables given.

The beautiful festival of lights (the Diwali) on the last day of the Hindu year is too well-known for description. Not so well-known is the fact that the little festal "ghee" lights have a distinct purpose, apart from the ordinary one of illumination; they are to light the way for the Goddess of Fortune.

Dire misfortune awaits the owners of the unlighted house, if the goddess by chance descends in her chariot to discover the reason of the lights not being there.

Two other customs, which introduced in Western countries might prove useful precedents, insist that a wife on a visit to her parents must be re-escorted home the first time she visits them either by the husband or some male member of his house, or she remains there for ever; and in certain communities, the Patel and Patidar ones for instance, the parents of a married daughter have to supply her with her clothes all her life, exactly as if she were still a maiden under their protection. It is the custom, also, of your true Indian lady never to repeat the name of her husband, and in this connection an extraordinary contretemps occurred, quite recently, at a certain wayside station.

A respectable Brahmin woman got down from a third class compartment, which had no bath-room arrangements, for a few minutes, and was unfortunately left behind by the train: still more unfortunately her husband was asleep in the compartment at the time, and thus the weeping lady was completely stranded.

The usual crowd collected, but nothing would make the wife repeat her husband's name.

The station master, also a Hindu, respecting her prejudices, finally wired along the line her caste and description, and as there was also a husband with a missing wife at the junction ahead, this faithful Hindu wife rejoined her husband, having obeyed the Hindu scriptures that say that God's name, the King's name, and the husband's name must never be repeated in public.

Most orthodox Hindu husbands as well as wives will never repeat each other's names: there is a superstition that this will bring about the early death of one or the other.

CHAPTER IX

In a Maharaja's Courtyard

THE Western world reads about Maharajas, Mahatmas, Brahmins, Pundits, Shastris, and—a sharp descent—of the untouchables at the very bottom of the social classes.

But in between these classes is a medley of other classes, completely different one from the other, who neither intermarry, nor eat in the same house even with each other. They have but one single thing in common, that of being an Indian.

Let the reader pass with the writer through the courtyard of an Indian prince, and meet some of these intermediate classes, and gain some insight into the lives of a number of Indians whom few of the Western world will ever know.

Seated at the *zenana-dodi*—door—is the Arab Jemadar, who is head of the Arabs who guard the entrance to the zenana. This one is typical of his kind, fussy and often irritable, but has a heart of gold. He is past-master at the art of anecdote-telling and there is always one in which generosity shines out as the supreme virtue, and he himself, though poor, is one of these generous souls.

Like most Arabs, he can sing and dance, but his dancing days were over when he grew a paunch, and topped the scale at fifteen stone.

He rules his Arabs with a rod of iron, and they are occasionally at daggers drawn, literally as well as figuratively.

He sleeps as befitting an Arab, with one eye open and the writer has seen him come to his feet from deepest sleep with dagger, drawn from cummerbund, in hand when someone to test him, deliberately dropped a book close to where his head lay on the stone floor.

He is a splendid cook and when guests are expected, he is generally in full charge of the Moghul kitchen. He is expert at making sherbets, " attahs "—scents—and, with some regret one must note, tonics for dilapidated youths.

He is a master of magic—though the Koran looks on this with disfavour—and knows many charms; his most famous ones being the cure of scorpion stings by commanding the pain to come down the limb and disappear at the tip of finger or toe. He cures toothache by driving a bit of wood into the ground with certain incantations. The writer often found a swollen cheeked patient or a victim of a scorpion-sting, obeying injunctions: for his cures are supposed to be efficacious and he does them not for money, but for love of humanity.

He told the writer that when he was a boy his mother fed him with roasted scorpion tails, and that no scorpion poison has since had any effect on his system.

He added that many an Arab mother did this; carefully, and wisely, refraining, however, from informing their children what they were eating: but readers must accept this tale very cautiously, for when the writer enquired further about the matter from a young Arab fresh from Arabia, he appeared to be seriously annoyed.

The Jemadar loves gossip, but it is never spiteful.

He has little respect for the fair sex: possibly the zenana has got too much on his nerves. He told the writer with conviction and sincerity, that it was one of the saddest truths of life, that the best men invariably drew the worst wives in the matrimonial lottery.

His faithfulness to his salt is unquestioned.

He was once a "Khalifatist," but his Arabs, straight from Arabia, gave him a very different version to the one he had read in the vernacular extremist papers and in his own expressive phrase, his "stomach now burns" at the money he gave to the Angora fund for the Khalif.

In the courtyard, in an office all his own, even more important than the Arab Jemadar, is the Huzuri, one of the men nearest to the Maharaja: holder of the privy purse.

He keeps the Prince's private accounts, and has an accessibility that is envied by even the Dewans of States.

The Huzuri feels his own importance, one sees that, he walks pompously and views the world with self-satisfaction; and tradesmen and visitors of the smaller kind fawn upon him as sole arbiter of their fate.

He wears spotlessly clean, white, flowing garments, and round his head is a neat, small turban in tightly wound muslin.

The Huzuri boys and Putta-vallas (literally—belt-bearers—peons, of whom more anon) are directly under him and he rules them with a rod of iron.

It is only in front of the Maharaja that any Huzuri ever appears meek.

He is honest and faithful to his master, but the dexterity with which he gets himself out of a difficult situation, and puts the man he dislikes in one of the worst has in it the elements that might well earn the envy of the present-day politician.

He is, generally, a Rajput, or a mixture of Rajput and Khavas, and though he is a conservative in his home, he is very fond of food served in correct English style, having visited Europe with his master. He is a great admirer of all things European, and often dilates on the busy English people: drawing an invidious comparison between them and Indians. The English people, he told his men, had little time to spare, and he never saw them talking or loitering on the road like they did in India.

Outside the Huzuri's office or the dressing rooms of the prince, sit the huzuri boys, standing when the great ones of the court pass, clothed in perfectly fitting clothes, and in their brightly coloured turbans is pinned the gold-crested miniature of their master, the Maharaja.

These boys have now, been more or less, replaced by a modern innovation—the *aide-de-camps*.

The duties of the "huzuri" boys are many and varied, from that of assisting in the dressing of their prince, looking after his clothes and jewels and writing minor notes, to the holding of his spittoon and the putting on or off of his boots. Fearing no one but their master, they carry all responsibilities lightly, living to the full the motto: "eat, drink and be merry, for to-morrow we die."

For they die often as far as their dignity is concerned: often superseded, many times degraded. But they have a splendid time while their day lasts: accompanying their master on his many travels; gaining much of largesse, and shining in the reflected glory of their master. They are generally Rajputs: often the same clan as the Maharaja himself or distant relatives.

Their forefathers were once large landlords, but the

coming of too many sons has split up the large landed property to mere fields; and within a few generations, the Maharaja's once powerful sirdars become petty landholders, glad to take any sort of post at the court of their kinsman: to bask in his smiles or wilt under his frowns, provided they taste again of the lost grandeur of their past ancestors.

As their posts are, more or less, created ones, they, who are so easily replaced, are never missed.

The Ganjar or barber is one of the indispensable people of life.

He is considered a low-class man; he cannot enter kitchens, and water cannot be drunk from his hands.

One is confronted with a strange contradiction here: for it is the barber who massages, pinches and squeezes the body of the most sacred person in the State; that of His Highness himself; and the writer has seen him at the table of, at least, one modern prince, bringing in the hot, unleavened bread on the palm of his hard hand, to be slapped down on the heavy silver trays. His ordinary duties of hair-cutting, shaving and cutting of nails down to the very quick, are as nothing to his duties of torch-bearer and wag.

It is his age-old privilege to bear a torch, either in a procession, in his gayest attire, or at a station or wayside place when the Maharaja arrives after sunset, lighting up the inky darkness with bright splotches of colour, and making a scene of almost barbaric splendour: from the skin bottle containing sweet seasamum oil in his left hand he replenishes his torch from time to time, when its brilliance tends to grow dim.

He is somewhat of a dandy where clothes are concerned

with his neatly buttoned short coat, his long loin cloth and his tightly wound turban, and the light from his torches brings into shining prominence every sheen of silk, every glisten of gold or glint on jewelled buttons, including him with the royal people whose way he lights—an unforgettable picture. The barber is a trained wag and the melancholy of his face,—Indian barbers are trained not to laugh,—misleads the uninitiated only.

His presence in the servants' quarters is always the herald of peals of laughter, in which he himself is never known to join.

He, too, is a faithful fellow, and though the means of killing are so readily at hand, the writer was told that it has never been known, even in the lawless days, of a barber having murdered his patron. He is very versatile: some of them have learnt how to shingle, and to shampoo, the use of ice lotions, and the trimming of a moustache in true Charlie Chaplin manner.

But they prefer the old greased ringlets; the long moustaches deftly twisted and tied up with something resembling a chinstrap round the ears at night, to induce the correct martial sweep, that Princes favour no more.

Yet it must be a very modern Indian still, to sacrifice the most coveted possession of an Indian male: his moustache; which is shaved off only during a period of mourning.

More often than not, gossiping with the Huzuri boys, are the peons—putta-vallas—of any and every caste, except that of the untouchable.

When they walk through the bazaar in their red turbans edged with gold, in their white uniforms with the red bands from shoulder to waist on which are the badges of their office in silver, or gold: their red loin cloths tied coquettishly to droop low over their right hip, they always attract attention.

The peons have their own methods of extracting tips; no name goes before the Huzuri without the whisper of largesse. They become disgracefully ragged together when a question of new clothes comes up, taking the heart out of all opposition, or proposers of economic cuts: the suddenness alone, of their dilapidated dress giving them away. They are fond of dainties, and not above sampling their master's food when chance throws a casual tiffin-basket their way.

When the Maharaja goes anywhere as a guest, they eat far more than he does, and their demands at the kitchen are often couched in so ambiguous a manner as to leave the impression that it is the Maharaja himself who is perpetually hungry.

Their methods of evading work, if published in book-form, would run into several volumes, and be, of its kind, unique.

The writer remembers one humorous instance of this evasion; she once gave a set of dusters to each separately; and, to be sure they were kept clean, she insisted on each man bringing his set to her every night. This scheme appeared an excellent one, till the accidental discovery that one set of these dusters, set religiously apart, neatly folded and spotlessly clean, and never used, was brought for the nightly inspection. They are never at a loss for an explanation, and if driven in a corner, disarm one by meekly pleading forgetfulness.

It is hard to find their good points, but they are obedient on occasion: post letters without removing the stamps—

though sometimes a day or two late—and when it is the only way to secure a peaceful life they work.

One must make way here for the " Poojari," or priest, who is perforce a Brahmin. You must not touch him, or he will be obliged to bathe again as he has to arrange the various things necessary for the Maharaja's prayers (*pooja*[1]).

In the beautiful room of marble, set apart for prayers, he places on one sandal-wood seat the picture of the family deity, the scented *agar-batti*—incense-sticks; the little silver receptacle to hold the ghee and cotton-wick, the silver bell, the pot of water with its quaint spoon, and the silver tray filled with jasmine, roses or oleanders. The first two flowers are offerings to the sun, and one by one in a silver-spoon of water to the tune of the " Gayatri Mantra " the sun-god accepts them: the second, beloved flower of Mahadeva, the great-god, are offered to Him.

On another sandal-wood seat facing this one, the Maharaja sits to prayers, and the *poojari* places the soft woollen *asanas*, over mats of dab-grass, prescribed by his religion. The priest in loose loin cloth, his sacred thread standing out in white relief from shoulder to waist on his dark shining body, his bare head shaven except for the lock of hair at the back of his head which is tied in a knot: his forehead smeared with sandal-wood, insignia of his own morning prayers, is rarely seen thus by the European, who sees him at mundane times when wearing his ordinary clothes: a coat, a *dhoti*—loin cloth—or loose trousers, and a small turban with the gold side higher than the other.

The priest avoids shoes, if possible, but he has a pair of

[1] The modern Maharaja is discarding this old custom.

slippers, the toes of which turn up at the ends, and one can only see them lying outside the Durbar steps ; for no true Hindu wears shoes either in the palace or the courtyard of a king.

The priest is one of the most important of men, indispensable at all religious ceremonies, and these are many. It is he who knows exactly what to do when the planets are unfavourable, who fixes the days necessary for fasting and the prayers necessary for propitiation.

We have already recounted his business of looking up an auspicious letter to start the name of a child, and his science enables him to tell his clients whether the hour of birth is an auspicious one or not, and how to ward off the impending evil if it is not : whether the child will bring misfortune to the father or grandfather—the mother hardly counts—and the rites necessary to be performed to prevent this calamity.

The writer knows of an instance where a royal baby born under an unpropitious sign was not shown to the father or grandfather until a month and a quarter had passed.

It is the priest again who compares the horoscopes of those about to wed.

Few Hindu parents, ancient or modern, will venture to question the Batji's[1] dictum.

At the opening of a new house, it is he again, who recites the necessary incantations that will drive away any evil spirits in need of a habitation, who propitiates the spirits of any whose abodes may have been ruthlessly disturbed in the process of building, and who engineers the house-warming feast where visitors partake of the expiation-feast

[1] Batji-priest.

necessary, to prevent the sin of the killing of insect-life during the process of building, falling on the owner alone.

The priest is a man of many parts, and it seems an irony of fate that with all this inner knowledge at his disposal, he himself is not always able to have, or to hold, the fortune that he invokes for others.

The working maid-servants belong to the zenana proper, but they are part of the inner courtyards. They are a noisy lot of women, some of them far from clean, but very hard working.

They rise at 4 o'clock in the morning, summer or winter, to churn the curdled buffaloes' milk that makes the butter afterwards to be made into *ghee*. They must finish their churning early to get through the day's work; for after four o'clock when their slack time commences, it is not considered auspicious to churn butter: butter-churning after four o'clock in the evening brings "heaviness" to the Maharaja.

The maid-servants are gross eaters and have no regular hours either for meals or work.

They belong mostly to the "Khavas" caste, a caste that has lax ideas about the sacredness of the marriage bond, which is made or broken very easily.[1]

The Brahmin priests, however, officiate; but at the first marriage only: all forth-coming marriages being celebrated in a quaint fashion: the woman puts a pot of water in her prospective husband's house, and on his lifting it up, the new marriage is ratified.

[1] This applies to Khavas Menials. The writer knows of Khavases who follow implicitly the Rajput way of living and the Rajput code of morals.

Strangely enough this marriage is also counted legal and it takes some trouble to annul it. It is to be supposed that a class whose ideas of morality are so elastic are not capable of conjugal fidelity; but whilst they live with a man they are rarely unfaithful to him.

It is a class that cannot change its views on life easily, and these views are necessarily restricted by the very narrowness of their little lives.

European standards of cleanliness are not easily acquired by them, and however perfect they may be in their powers of imitation, any relaxation of vigilance, even for a day, means a falling back to their own old methods. They are, nevertheless, very willing creatures with any amount of endurance where hard work is concerned; and in their own walk of life, absolutely indispensable to the mistresses they serve.

The Bhoee is the water-bearer. He brings the palace drinking water from a specially reserved well, and is always accompanied by an Arab with a drawn sword.

He carries the water in covered brass-pots, held in suspended rope receptacles attached to the two ends of a bamboo carried over his shoulder.

The water is the most important thing in an Indian household: not for its utility alone, but because of the belief that any profane touch of the water will mean the religious defilement of a whole household.

Water touched by a person of another religion: water touched by a member of another community or a lower caste, or by one in whose house or family there has been a recent death or birth: water touched by a woman in her menses are all alike taboo to your orthodox Hindu, who will thirst to death rather than drink of this forbidden water.

The " Bhoee " fills a great many number of water pots for the royal household to drink during a day, but his task is considerably lightened by many leisurely hours of rest; for he waits long, and gossips much, outside the zenana courtyard, before the dilatory maid-servants find time to come out with their own brass-pots, to take over the fresh water.

The water-carrier dresses in clean white garments, and wears a coloured turban with long flowing ends; he has rings of brass or silver, according to his wealth, in his ears.

His duty ends with the bringing of the drinking water. In modern palaces pipes are laid on in every room, but, in this strange land of many contradictions, it may not come as so great a surprise as might be expected, to learn that even a high class Brahmin, who would shudder to eat or drink anything in the establishment of another, may drink pipe-water.

The " Bhoee " holds a very important place in all highly orthodox Hindu establishments, but his trustworthiness does not appear to be above suspicion in Royal Households, as the ubiquitous Arab and his sword proclaim.

The " Charan " is an extempore poet, attached to every Indian court, and his curse or blessing is believed to possess power.

To offend a " Charan " is still considered by the majority of Indians, rich and poor alike, a misfortune.

In olden days when bad debts were difficult to collect,

the ubiquitous " Charan " instituted himself the court of appeal.

For a large sum of money, he took up his position in front of the defaulter's house, refusing to eat or drink till the debt was paid. On the third day, if the debt remained unpaid, the " Charan was supposed to stab himself to death with a dagger, the idea being that the sin of a " Charan's " death would fall on the obstinate defaulter. It is on record that few debtors allowed matters to go so far, but there are cases where " Charans " have been allowed to die, and have actually died. In this instance the writer remembers a case that occurred quite recently in Mount Abu, when a member of this caste who had some grievance against a Sirdar of Sirohi, and had appealed in vain for Agency intervention, entered the office of the Agent to the Governor-General, and with his petition in his left hand ran his sword through his throat with his right.

The " Charan " varies, from the meaner type who wander about scaring respectable people by their curses into giving them money and food, to the quaint minstrels with their one-stringed gourd-instrument—the *tamboora*—who gain money by their singing, up to the cream of them all, refined poets; who in liquid tones, recite or read out reams of flowing poetry at the big durbars of the Maharaja, praising, in no scanty terms, the generosity they hope, so sincerely, to partake of at the end of the Durbar.

This latter type is often an important match-maker: for he carries,—for a fee,—descriptions of lovely bride or noble bridegroom from one court to another; and his wit and ready ingenuity gain for him many friends as well as largesse.

Like the court jester of old, no ceremony of address binds him: and he is allowed a good deal of license, daring to say much, even to-day, that no other courtier would or could dare, and he often uses his liberty for the good of others.

It was, at one time, considered obligatory on the part of all Indian princes to feed the " Charans " of their own or neighbouring States; but some of the " Charans "—especially the women—have proved a veritable nuisance; and this legacy of obligation from the past no longer conjures up any conception of the old grandeur when " Charans " were counted of the immortals; and the " Charan " can no longer count upon his free meals.

The " Chōpdar " (herald) is another picturesque figure seen at all the big durbars, and at the nightly courts where the officers of the State come to pay their respects to the Maharaja.

He holds a gold-mounted mace: his turban is of gold cord shot with green with jaunty gold tassels hanging over at one side: he wears tight-fitting pantaloons, surmounted by a coat of white, and his gay gold-tissue loin cloth is tied in a knot at the side, over a dagger with a jewelled hilt.

As the Maharaja alights from his carriage or car the herald precedes him to the door of the durbar, clearing the way, which is already cleared, with his drawn-out cry *agar—meherbaan—salaam*, " At a distance—His Highness—Salaam." Standing aside as the Maharaja passes, bent to the ground in obsequiousness, he repeats his call.

He calls out as each newcomer enters and salaams: and again when the Maharaja rises to leave his court.

Sometimes at a court there are several "Chōpdars" together: the musical cry is taken up one after the other making a musical medley not without effect: "Salute O City! His Kindness."

The "Chōpdar's" duties are varied: he takes out the durbar lists for signature: on these are written the names of all sirdars and notables of a State and their presence is indispensable at a court.

It is his duty to introduce and usher in all new poets and singers; unceremoniously cutting their performances short at the slightest sign of boredom from his royal master, and introducing others to the Presence.

It is indeed a happy poet or singer,—man or woman,—who, winning the favour of the Maharaja's interest, is allowed to finish poem or song.

In processions the "Chōpdar" walks at the side of the Maharaja's carriage, the very emblem of pomp and circumstance.

But his fortune depends upon his voice, and when it loses its bell-like quality, the dignified post of herald, is also lost and he no longer holds any position at court.

The dancing-girl, subject of endless criticism and discussion, belongs to the night.

She wears voluminous skirts, a tight-fitting heavily embroidered bodice, covered with a little jacket and a transparent costly *sari*. But when she is no longer a virgin, she discards the jacket for a *choli*. Her boldness is part of her audacious fascination: her mouth is full of betel and her roving eyes seek out likely prey.[1]

[1] This describes the older dancing-girl, who has lost her innocence.

She is a startling type whose greatest insincerity is in her life-like imitation of sincerity, which many an Indian aristocrat has found out too late: your out-and-out courtesan will ever pose as the most faithful of mistresses to the man whose favour she covets.

This copying of the great emotions extends to her musicians even, who, sitting in a half-circle behind her, are true to type: if you see one lot, you have seen them all.

There is the man with the drum who would appear to admire her vivaciously: his eyes never leave her face; he evidently knows that the weakness of human nature is to be fascinated most with that which fascinates others.

At times, as if involuntarily, he emits a rapturous: "*Waah waah*"—well done! well done! and shakes his head as if lost in complete ecstasy.

There are those who play the string instruments, always in dreamy abstraction; eyes cast down, and heads, if they wag at all, part of this assumed, intense melancholy engendered by a hopeless love; falling to their breasts at last in reveries so profound as to partake almost of stupor.

Sometimes the rôles are changed and we have the string instrumentalists vivacious and in raptures of delight, and now it is the turn of the man who plays the drum to be intensely melancholy.

Vatsyana who taught the dancing-girl his famous eighty-four arts of how to collect money and cheat, cannot escape full liability, even though the last verses of his book insist on assuring his readers that these arts, taught by him, were done so with the sole idea of proving their futility.

"Be sure," said Vatsyana with a wisdom worthy of a better cause, in his chapter of notorious advice to dancing-girls,[1] "to be friendly with policemen and magistrates. You might find this friendship some day, useful."

[1] The reader should be careful to distinguish between the dancing-girl (Nayaka) proper, and the modern Indian danseuse. It is a happy feature of present-day Indian thought on these things, that the beautiful Indian dance is no longer delegated to the dancing-girl; and that Indian ladies of breeding and culture are dancing now in public without the social oblivion that would have been theirs half a century ago.

CHAPTER X

In an Indian Bazaar

STRANGE place of indescribable smells; pungent spices, dried pulses, assafoetida, scented gums, hot *ghee* and oil, and others too unpleasant to mention, no tale of India could be complete without a picture of some of the inmates of a truly Indian bazaar.

The brightly coloured wares, red and saffron cloths, outside the shop of a dyer catch and hold the eye: there is no red like this outside of India, no yellow so yellow. The dyer-class claims to be an off-shoot of the Kshatriya or warrior caste,—his name corrupted into Khatri,—but, unfortunately for his assumption, the dyer—Khatri—is included in the "Nava-jat"—nine castes—of the Vaisya or merchant class, and is invited to their caste-dinners.

The Khatri's class is a highly conservative one, no Khatri marries outside his own circle; but his widow, unlike those of other conservative classes, is allowed to remarry.

His art of mixing colours, those bright, gay colours of the East, is well known to the Western world. But he possesses another and finer art which unfortunately is not so well known: the making, and dyeing of crinkled cloth of intricate designs in little patches and circles of colour.

To do this work he lets the nail on the third finger of his left hand grow very long, and this helps him the more easily to pinch up hundreds of little bits of cloth in the correctest of patterns and to tie them with fine thread.

The whole cloth is then dipped in dye; the tied-up bits alone retaining the ground colour; and, so perfectly are they tied, that the pattern is almost perfect.

The dyer sells his work still tied, but a gentle pull brings the threads apart, displaying in all its beauty the wonderful work.

Some of the larger of these cloths take from two to three months to prepare, and are by reason of this labour, costly.

But the Khatri, though a hard-working man, will never be able to get rich: for, and this is a real tragedy in India, these simple artisans of India are invariably exploited—by their countrymen most of all—hardly making the barest of profit; thus encouraging the slip-shod work one associates these days with Indian work.

In separate streets altogether are the workers in metal—the Kansaras.

The Kansara is seen, from sunrise to sunset in his little shop, beating metal into pots, large and small, and the ring of metal on metal, resounds through the street.

This beating of copper is an arduous task, and the big fire over which he spends part of the time, adds to his labour when the days grow hot, and the temperature stands at over a hundred and sixteen.

He develops wrinkles very soon, for by nightfall his eyes are always tired, and he works by the measurement of his own correct eye alone, making articles of various sizes: large brass and copper pots for filling water; smaller ones, with a tin-lining done by men in another street, for milk; trays of copper or silver; drinking goblets, cups; cooking utensils and ladles of every description; all beaten out by hand, and so beautiful as to make one wonder why the princes do not patronise him more.

The Kansara is of the conservative class, and his widow cannot remarry.

Past him are the sweet-meat sellers, always dirty, always greasy, with the sweet-meat they themselves have made, piled before them; more often than not, covered with flies.

Sometimes they are seen frying *jellebees* made of fermented flour, run through a hole in a coco-nut shell into large cauldrons of hot oil, or stirring milk in large iron pots.

Then there is a separate street for the cobblers who are more or less untouchables, where the orthodox Hindu is concerned: for your orthodox Hindu considers leather impure, and tanners and cobblers share in the impurity.

There is, again, a separate street where tailors sit and sew; with the silk-clothes that will adorn some great lady or noble, held nimbly between their toes, side by side with the country-spun shirt of some low-born man.

Another street full of the scent of flowers, where flower-sellers display garlands of jasmine and rose for the necks of some loved one; idol of gold or man or woman.

It is close to the street where the sellers of betel-leaves and spices sit making up the little green three-cornered betel packets, filled with lime, and held together by a clove.

A nation of children, these Indians of an India that is really India, with the flowers round their necks, who will buy and chew these betel-leaves, dyeing lips and teeth alike a yellowy-red, living happily for the day; careless of the morrow.

CHAPTER XI

The Untouchables

OF all the strange anomalies of life, the strange one of the untouchables of India would make a tale of the saddest reading, but for the strange inconsistencies, that make for a humour not wholly grim.

The Western world may be surprised to learn that there are two main classes of untouchables; the one considering itself as badly defiled by the touch of the other, as the orthodox classes are by that of any untouchable.

Of these two classes: the superior (God save the word!) untouchables are the "Deds": and a very sturdy, independent class they are, one that views with deep distrust all attempts to break down barriers of caste, scenting in this new movement no special advantage to themselves.[1]

And this, though it does not still apply to the "Deds" educated on English lines, does, still, to the "Deds" proper: they who work in gardens, who are labourers, who build the houses that Brahmins and Rajas live in, after the necessary purificatory rites.

These "Deds" are an exemplary class; one could wish them unchanged.

They are very hard-working, and their girls work side

[1] This was written in 1929.

by side with them and have a higher market value than their men-folk.

In the marriage-market, they fetch high prices by reason of this, and are sold, literally sold, to prospective parents-in-law; a statement that will appear appalling to a European, but for the fact that the girl herself is not an unwilling participator in many, if not all, of the bargains.

The average price of an ordinary " Ded " girl is about Rs. 800—£60 to-day—and it is fixed by the " Nāt," viz., the caste-men.

The writer once suggested to a lamenting mother, that the Maharaja might be asked to break up this custom, and was met with a horrified protest from the mother. Certainly not, the " Nāt " knew best.

The mother herself had two sons; but she hoped to be able to recover the money paid for their brides by the good price she was sure to get for her three strong good-looking daughters.

When the daughters get their first babies, a certain amount of the purchase-money goes back to the bride-groom's house: custom obliging the mother to give large presents.

When a " Ded " girl becomes a widow, the parents may claim her back in their house, and get her remarried by paying back the purchase money: sometimes the new bridegroom, especially if the girl is good-looking, helps by paying the purchase-money.

Sometimes the parents-in-law are loth to return their daughter-in-law; if she is a hard worker, this means the loss of a wage-earner of six to ten annas a day.[1]

[1] With this apparently small wage, the " Ded " lives, pays large sums for his bride, and few girls are without gold jewelry.

The matter then goes up before the "Nāt" whose decision is binding.

These girls appear extremely happy and know full well their high market value.

They are noted for their chastity and are adepts at the art of controlling husbands.

The "Ded" woman, being a wage-earner, has the means of flying off to her parents' house, whenever her husband shows signs of proving difficult; and a very dejected husband goes after her and brings her back, usually on her own terms.

It is from the "Ded" class that many Hindu servants of the "Sahib-lok" are recruited, and it was for this reason, more than from the defilement of the "Sahib", that, until quite recently, Indian princes were reluctant about accepting hospitality from Englishmen in India.

Food eaten from the hands of an untouchable makes for impurity of the highest degree, and it takes a whole religious ceremony, painful penances, and a sacrifice to get ritually right.

The touch alone, however, loses its evil effect by bathing, and, if bathing is not possible for some time, the sprinkling on of water, in which gold has been put, will restore purity. The writer vividly remembers a "Ded" woman, her gardener, whose spade had been touched by a sweeper, loosen her gold ear-ornament, drop it into a pot of water and sprinkle her "defiled" spade with this water.

In the diary of one of the oldest converts to Christianity, the writer has been told by his son, it is recorded that about the time of the Great Indian Mutiny year, the "Deds" were considered lower than the pariah-dogs. A dog might go to the house of a "Ded" and eat his food, and the other Hindus would have no scruples whatsoever in touching that dog, but they would never touch the " Ded " himself. Even his very shadow and his foot-prints in the dust were considered defiling.

In those days, in certain villages round about Gujarat, the " Deds " and the " Bhangis ",–Sweepers,–were forced to drag leafy branches of trees behind them in order to obliterate their foot-marks, and to cry at the top of their voices : " way—way—to pass—please."

It was the missionaries of those days who changed all this : credit must be given to them alone.

Amazing to relate : if a Hindu touched by a " Ded " were touched by a Mahomedan, the contamination went out of him : two minuses making a plus.

Even those Deds who have become Christians,—and there are thousands in Gujarat,—still retain many of their old customs, e.g., keeping " Tulsi "—balsam—plants in their houses, and worshipping them ; the retention of the custom of child marriages[1] and, the same Indian Christian assures the writer, the singing of obscene songs on the occasion of marriage and other feasts.

The writer was also told that one of these well-to-do converts was asked as to the reason why he, a Christian, kept the " Tulsi " plant in his house ; he was said to have replied that he wished to be absolutely on the safe side : if the God of the Christians did not save him, he might yet be saved by the God of Tulsi.

In former times, a Ded was not allowed to ride a horse through a village, nor was he allowed to carry an open umbrella, nor wear a modern coat, nor a pair of shoes. Neither was he, at one time, allowed to live in good houses.

[1] The Sarda bill is preventing these to-day.

The Deds of Gujarat are generally wealthy: by this old arbitrary law they ran a good risk of losing all their money: for Indians of old invariably kept their money hidden in their houses.

The Deds observe very rigidly all the principal festivals of both the Hindus and the Mahomedans; and where there are many Christians, they observe Christmas also: their women dress in gay and costly clothes and wear many ornaments on the Hindu festival of "Diwali," and you will find them as gaudily dressed in the forefront of the Moharrum processions.

The Bhangi or sweeper class, is far inferior to that of the Ded. The work of the sweeper, his physique, his intelligence are all alike of a mean order; but whether it is fate or man that has made him so sorry a specimen of humanity, is a debatable point.

That his lot is pitiable is undoubtedly true: though like all lots there are some bright spots for his small consolation.

His drumming is required at festivals. In Indian States he beats the drums at the head of processions. Whenever a proclamation is to be made throughout a town or village, it is the sweeper who does it with a beat of his drum.

The writer was told, somewhat naïvely, by an official, that the presence of the sweeper cleared the road more effectively than a posse of police.

A Sadhu friend of hers travelled in a crowded train, a whole third-class compartment to himself, because the other occupant happened to be a sweeper.

Here the sweeper scored, but not so lucky was that other sweeper of the writer's who had to miss three trains at a junction to wait for an empty compartment, and who was obliged to walk up from Abu Road to Mount Abu, because he was not allowed to sit in the motorbus by his fellow passengers.

Like the Ded, the sweeper has a rigid caste system and the " Patel ",—head of the Nāt,—has the last say in any matter.

Neither he nor the Ded is allowed in Hindu or Jain temples.

Manu has been blamed for the rigidity of the caste in this respect, but Manu's ruling does not give any clue as to the present-day theory of defilement. Manu, meaning well like all reformers, in his desire to protect the weak, enunciated a theory; that a man with an undeveloped brain should not be made responsible for the acts inspired by that brain.

The Shudra,—thus Manu's dictum,—can do no wrong because he is unable to distinguish between what is right and what is wrong ; therefore he who does not sin requires no sacraments ; has no religious ceremonies to perform, and may take up certain duties only if he feels willing, and able to perform them.

And in Manu 5, 127, Manu re-emphasizes that conduct alone determines the caste of a man.

A thousand would be reformers may burn the laws[1] of Manu, but it is still debatable whether one who meant so well of his kind, is really responsible for the present-day impasse.

The Bhangis worship a Pir called Ramo Pir, and the Deds have their own temples and " mahants "—priests.

To add to the bathos, the sweepers hold themselves

[1] This was done quite recently in Bombay.

the direct descendants of Rukhis or Rishis—seers—and they will not eat except at their own places, lest a piece of food falling to the ground give to the owner of that ground, the religious merit of the eater and his noble ancestors.

Whilst on the question of untouchables: certain aborigines like the Bhils, the Todas, etc., are also counted untouchables by the Aryan Hindu. The drinking water of all aborigines is taboo for them: though their touch alone does not always defile.

The " Vaagadi " is of an aboriginal class, and though he dresses on occasion with due grandeur, his general aspect is far from grand: he is dirty, his hands caked with much mud, and his skin oiled by dirt and perspiration.

He believes, with some degree of justice,–in India at any rate,–that washing, not dirt, is the ruin of clothes; so he keeps one set apart for gala days alone and on these rare occasions he washes. His other set comprising a shirt and dhoti—loin cloth—he wears till it falls to tatters on his person.

He earns his living by the occasional sweat of a brow which is never wiped.

He grows little patches of water-melons, sugar melons, cucumbers and pumpkins of all shapes. His greatest antipathy in life is the porcupine: an antipathy that can be shared by all those gardeners who grow these four things so favoured of the spiked one.

The responsibilities of marital life sit loosely on this class, and the habit of placing the care of a crowd of children on to the father—or *vice versa*—is a common habit of erring wives and husbands of this class.

The Vaagadis live in rude huts, made of mats of grass,

on their little patches, in company with pariah dogs, fowls, goats and occasionally pigs, and like the gypsies of the Western world they are not above thieving.

They set at naught the rules of hygiene, but their children, apart from a kind of perpetual hay-fever and its consequent nose-dripping, appear remarkably healthy.

One sees these fat black naked babies rolling about the roads as prolific as the melons their fathers grow.

The Vaagadis do as little work as they possibly can, trusting to fate to feed them and their children.

They are even too lazy to protect their little bits of land against the raids of the porcupines, and even when they are eaten out of house and home, rather than take the trouble to repair the damage, they prefer to start life again as beggars pure and simple.

CHAPTER XI

The Education of Girls

THE educationist in this country could not have better material to work on than the Indian girl. She possesses all the qualities that make the ideal pupil: imitation, a good memory, and a loving heart; qualities that are at once her fortune and misfortune.

The word misfortune is used advisedly.

Not to every girl in India comes the ideal teacher. Sometimes the Indian teacher is against progress as spelt by Western ideals, and sometimes the English teacher ruthlessly destroys what he or she cannot replace: forgetting that it is not every Western idea that will grow in Indian soil, and that imitation carried to excess makes for mediocrity.

Memory may retain undesirable things, and that very tenderness of a heart which can be an asset may accept impressions which may destroy for ever, any clear outline of character.

And there is one great gift, with few exceptions, that is still denied by the gods to the Indian girl: the gift of perseverance.

The mind of the average Indian girl is like a screen on which must always be thrown a fresh picture to keep up interest.

This strange incapacity of bringing a thought or act to its logical conclusion or fulfilment, is one of the greatest drawbacks that educationists of Indian girls have continually to combat.

The mind of the Indian girl has to be stimulated, restimulated and sometimes over-stimulated. She goes in for one thing, only to drop it for another more interesting, and this continues with few exceptions throughout her whole educational career.

Education, for its own sake, is a meaningless term to her. Education for the sake of a future position in life: for the adding to her value in the marriage market; for a hundred and one reasons, are listened to, appreciated at their proper value.

In the early days of the writer's own school, striving—and in those days it was indeed difficult—to make education for girls popular among the ordinary classes of Indian women, she had to descend the scale with a vengeance to bring home to them the value of education.

Most Indian women disliked the idea of school for their daughters.

Whilst they would willingly put the very small ones to school to get rid of the burden of looking after them, they would never do so with the older girls, whose absence from home added to their burden, already heavy, of house-keeping.

It seemed almost impossible to bring home to them the value of education.

The general answer was that their daughters were not to be teachers, but house-wives, and that it was too much waste of time—these hours at school.

The writer sent for some of the mothers, and agreed

on the face of it, that it would appear waste of time; but appealed for the mental upliftment of the race that would have educated mothers. A vain appeal—upliftment was a matter of fate.

When the writer pointed out that the present-day educated boy wanted as his partner in life an educated wife, they were considerably shaken, and gave way completely when it was added that business nowadays calling the husband away, the present method of having his letters opened, and read by an outsider was very unsatisfactory: would it not be more correct if the wife herself could read them and write the reply?

The initial difficulty surmounted, other difficulties arose.

The quick memory of the Indian girl made memorising easy, besides being the easiest method for both Indian teacher and pupil to make a display of knowledge, taught and learnt: the girl who read the quickest received generally the greatest praise from her teacher.

Careful analysis however proved that not only was the substance of what was read in the majority of cases not properly understood, but the girl was rarely able to give the most meagre of renderings of what she had read in her own language.

This latter drawback is still a serious obstacle in the education of girls. It prevents all originality: if not actually including want of originality.

In many cases the teachers themselves lack, in no small degree, the gift of remoulding a lesson in different words, and the vocabulary of certain vernacular dialects,—Gujarati for instance, that has to draw largely from Sanscrit to become any kind of classical prose,—being limited, adds to the difficulty. So it cannot be said, yet, that originality, initiative, or the power to think for themselves is a natural quality in the Indian girl.

Yet, one must in fairness emphasize, this is not due to dullness of mind, but rather laziness of mind. She follows, instinctively, the line of least resistance, and when mental effort may be too prolonged, or result in a combat, she avoids effort or combat.

In her own domain, that of the house, she has great qualities: a wonderful cook, a comptroller in its highest and most appreciated form; but as a mother, again, she follows the same path of least resistance, and her children are often spoilt.

Her social mistakes appear to be simply a confusing of issues when too much demand is made on her powers of judgment.

As instance of this: several Brahmin ladies are now eating meat against their innermost convictions, against every tenet of their creed, consoling themselves that this being the husband's wish, the merit of obedience outweighs the fault, if any, of the sacrificing of the dearest principles of their religion, nay of their very life.

At least one Brahmin lady told the writer that to be invited to the dinners of the Sahib-lok made it necessary for them to eat meat: this, to an English vegetarian, for whom, at the greatest of official dinners, a vegetarian menu is always provided, would point more than anything else to some strange, moral weakness.

A reaction, equally strange, will make for a tremendous upheaval of ethics, but it is difficult to prescribe a remedy. Each individual case requires its own diagnosis, and general advice may not entirely cover the ground.

But, undoubtedly, women's opinions, their cherished

ideals, at least, ought to be more carefully respected—even fostered—by their male-folk, not only helping to strengthen mildness of character, but for the prevention of the ultimate extreme when re-action occurs.

This is a lengthy digression from education proper. Returning to school and school hours, these are admittedly too long. But, these are inevitable: the Indian girl's school-life is already too short.

Among the conservative classes, the Brahmin or "Kunbi" (agriculturists) classes for instance, the girl is, more often than not, a mother at fourteen or fifteen; and school-days and girlhood are, for ever, over.

All educationists of girls, in India, feel this continual fight against time, and dare not remit a single of these relentless, sacred hours.

There are some cultured girls who carry on their education even after marriage, but they are in the minority: others do not return to school again except as widows: when study becomes for them a thing with an object in view; the getting into a teacher's preparatory class and passing through a training college. With the necessary teacher's certificate, she can then earn a living in a girls' school.

But the opportunity to study after marriage is slight: so whilst orthodox Hinduism requires her marriage before puberty,[1] which generally occurs in the Indian girl between the ages of twelve and fourteen, all advantage must be taken of the long hours.

At an age when a Western girl is still playing with her dolls, the little Indian girl is suckling her baby, a mother.

Only what she has learnt before this event, remains for

[1] This was written in 1929.

her to pass on to her child; little enough indeed. Her child, sometimes, accepts what she has to give, but more often accepts nothing—especially if it be a son who has learnt more in his two years of college life, than all his mother has ever learnt in hers.

Only the stern ethics of a religion that demands unqualified respect prevents her losing all influence over her child.

CONCLUSION

AND this is the India that is India, pulsating to a thousand different rhythms, laden with thoughts that are strangely alien and absolutely different to those of the Western world.

These tailors of India who despise the food of Indian kings: the low-caste menials who despise that cooked by cobblers: cobblers, again, who are contaminated by the food of Deds, and Deds who will not touch, let alone, eat with, a sweeper.

Is there a single thing here that we of the West can understand?

The genius that defies England to-day, is of England herself: a handful of Indians, educated on English lines—their papers are in English; their speeches imbued throughout with British ideas of democracy: hopelessly defiled, themselves, by all the ethics that make their own Hindu orthodoxy, which completely denies them, even to-day, the "darshana" of their old temples, and invites them no longer to the feasts of their own old caste.

Do they really speak for Indians and the heart of India? At the most they may claim they speak for the future of India: but still they represent a part, a very small part alone, of their huge country.

It is well for them to agitate for the rights of the untouchables; for they themselves, by association with those outside their caste, have also become to their own caste untouchables.

The heart of India has changed little during the centuries. Will it really change now by this vigorous impact of England, and things English?

The very vehemence with which the Indian agitator would deny the effect on himself from this impact is in itself an unwary admittance, that he is not untouched.

It is still too early to foretell with any certainty the future of India; whether India is really changeless, or whether in her modelling of herself on new lines, she will, like Japan and Turkey, try completely to annul all her old ideas and follow the methods of the West.

When history will set down, with the coldness of a century hence, what England has strived to do for India, then and then alone, will the world truly know, not only her mistake in this careless implanting of her own democratic ideas in the soil of an intensely conservative people; but the greatness, the liberality, and the magnitude of England, who having gained all, gave back all.

SOME RECENT REVIEWS OF BOOKS BY THE SAME AUTHOR

Mahatma Ram Das in his magazine, "The Vision," dated *October*, 1933.

THE PHILOSOPHY OF YOGA. Containing the mystery of spirit and the way to Eternal Bliss. By ELIZABETH SHARPE, Shri Krishna Nivas, Limbdi, Kathiawar.

This book of Yoga reveals the heights of mysticism to which the authoress has reached. So it is no wonder that this great work should issue from her inspired pen. The book divides mainly into two parts. The first part treats of the mystery of Yoga expounded in the Bhagvad Gita. As one goes through it one is subtly overpowered by its depth of thought, charm of idealism and purity and felicity of expression. Its every sentence is a distilled essence breathing the spirit of Truth. A few sentences from these pages quoted here would bear out the truth of the above observation:

"Every thought came to man through pain."

"Words are unable to hold the greatest thoughts, and thoughts at best are only to reflect, not able to capture pure Spirit."

. . . . . .

"What peace equal to that peace beyond the meagre powers of Understanding! The peace of realisation. And it is man's heritage."

"When the mind of man merges into the mind of God through Divine Affinity of thought, then can man realise the mind of God."

. . . . . .

Now the second part "The Chid Vilasom" is an exposition of Shakta Tantra. This as well is a fascinating garland of inspired gems of "purest ray serene." Here are some pearls:

"The soul is the Deity of the temple of the body. It is the making Divinity the essence of one's own soul."

"The whole moveable and immoveable universe are mirrored in the heart of man."

From the few extracts cited above, the reader can find out for himself the outstanding merit and beauty of the work THE PHILOSOPHY of Yoga. Everyone interested in the Yoga Philosophy should not fail to read this unique work.

The book is rightly dedicated by the authoress to her Guru, Shri Shanti Vijayjee of Mount Abu—a Mahatma of wide-spread fame.—"The Vision," dated *October*, 1933.

The book is esentially for the mystic, and for those to whom Hindu Philosophy as expounded by the Bhagvad Gita makes an appeal.—"The Civil and Military Gazette," dated *13th August*, 1933.

"United India and Indian States," dated New Delhi, *4th November*, 1933.

This book is one of a series of religious books, being issued in memory of the eldest grand-child of His Highness the Thakur Sahib of Limbdi. The series "aims at the spiritual education of the children of the Kshatriyas of India, who were once teachers of the Brahmins, hoping that once again they shall know, care more for and follow the great, pure religion of their ancestors, whence came all their power." The present book expounds the author's conception of the aim of Yoga, The Philosophy of Yoga, she writes, "aims not at super-natural powers, these are really natural to man, but at restoring to man a knowledge of ethics, leading back to the Original Purity that was Harmony." She has examined the teachings of the Gita in the light of this theory, striving to gather the main threads of thought and dropping all tangled ones. She has also availed herself of "Chid Vilasum" a rare old Sanscrit manuscript on Shakta Tantra. The earnest student of Yoga will no doubt welcome the little book as a lucid introduction to an abstruse subject and yet like Oliver he cannot help asking for more from the gifted author.

A.

Miss Elizabeth Sharpe has added to her list of publications by a book on a subject with which English people are not often acquainted. She has evidently studied the science of yoga, as expounded by the Bhagvad Gita, because her chapters are very analytical and show a deep knowledge of a very difficult subject. In her foreword she says:

"The book is one of a series of religious books in memory of the late K. S. Ram Rajendrasinhji, aged 14, eldest grandchild of that great soul, His Highness Thakore Sahib Shri Sir Daulat Sinhji, K.C.S.I., K.C.I.E., of Limbdi. These books aim at the spiritual education of the children of the Kshatriyas of India, who were once teachers of the Brahmins, hoping that once again they shall know, care more for and follow the great, pure religion of their ancestors, whence came all their power."

Buried in this little volume of profound thought and passionate sincerity are one or two theories which will provoke cutting criticism. One is contained in the appendix and is the theory that Christ and Krishna were originally one. The author some years ago made a list of the similar utterances of Christ and of Krishna. One can quite understand that this original theory is very unacceptable.—" The Illustrated Weekly of India," dated 11*th June*, 1933.

FINE TYPE OF INDIAN RULER

Woman's Picture of Limbdi Thakore Sahib

THAKORE SAHIB SHRI SIR DAULATSINGH OF LIMBDI. A Biography by ELIZABETH SHARPE, London. (John Murray). 7*s*. 6*d*.

It is doubtful whether the Thakore Sahib of Limbdi could have found a better biographer than his well-known Private Secretary, Miss Elizabeth Sharpe, who has had unique opportunities of studying a very fine type of Rajput character.

Anyone who has come in touch with His Highness must realise that the author has captured something of that healthy mental atmosphere which surrounds a fine old-fashioned type of gentleman-soldier, who now in his 64th year leads as full a life as many a man 20 years his junior.

We get some amusing stories about the Indian ruler's private life from his youth up. For instance, there was the time when he decided on a Hardwar pilgrimage, and having gone to bathe with a friend, found that his trousers had been stolen by a holy monkey. All efforts to persuade the monkey to eat grain and release the trousers failed, because he ate with one hand and held the coveted trousers with the other—finally tearing them to pieces and throwing them back at Dadbha, who had to return to Meerut in his bathing loincloth!

There were days when the young prince rode to Rajkot and back, a distance of 120 miles, through dacoit infested country—entirely alone and without fear. There was one occasion when he chatted with dacoits, who later in the day had a terrific battle with the Police Superintendent, three of the miscreants being killed. There are charming little stories of his unostentatious charity; of a favourite trick in going to a grain merchant and ordering food to be sent to a certain household without disclosing the donor.

Foolish Prejudices.

Over 30 years ago, His Highness went with a military contingent to the opening ceremony of the Federation of Australia, and the gentlemanly but firm way in which he met the racial prejudices of those days makes amusing reading in parts. There was, for instance, an unfortunate Sikh Indian officer who slept on deck of the *Dalhousie* a little over the British Officer's chalk line. The Troops Commander made a fuss, but later on the Captain of the ship (who seems to have been annoyed over the racial distinctions) ordered his lascars to sleep on this officer's reserved deck! A sense of humour with a vengeance.

The book shows in what high esteem His Highness holds the King Emperor, and there is a story about His Majesty which pays tribute to the King's remarkable memory about a small incident when he first met the Thakore Sahib. This loyalty accounts for the fact that it is the King Emperor's portrait that His Highness always sees in the morning when rising: and that he will never tear a postage stamp. There are boxes and boxes of used postage stamps in the palace, carefully stored and never destroyed.

The book also contains some picturesque little cameos of Limbdi to-day. The Thakore Sahib knows how improvident the ordinary ryot is, and to encourage him to stack his grass, he gives annually a rich turban of honour to the ryot who has the biggest stack.

The author says the Thakore Sahib rises in all climates at 3 a.m., and spends at least five hours daily at his prayers; and in spite of his age, he averages three hours at his Secretariat.

She adds in conclusion:

> "His own wants are very small. No prince in India spends less on his own person. He dresses always in simple, spotless, white muslin, with simple muslin head-dress. The rest of his attire is equally simple and unostentatious. His charity too is unostentatious: the extent and the lavishness of it, and the methods by which he ensures secrecy, are known, in full, only to the holder of his privy purse, and a few of his personal entourage. The greater part of the Thakore Sahib's private income goes entirely in charity."—"The Illustrated Weekly of India," dated *12th November*, 1933.

"The Illustrated Weekly of India," dated *4th March*, 1934.

THE TANTRIK DOCTRINE OF IMMACULATE CONCEPTION. By ELIZABETH SHARPE, F.R.G.S., F.R.E.S., M.R.A.S., F.B.E.E. (Rider). *4s. 6d.*

Miss Elizabeth Sharpe needs no introduction. This prolific writer is well known to Indian readers. She is a scholar of Hindu philosophy and religion and has written thought-provoking books like, "The Flame of God" and "The Philosophy of Yoga."

Moreover she has the distinction of being the Private Secretary to H.H. the Thakore Sahib of Limbdi. The above book, Miss Sharpe's latest, is culled from the Shakta-Kaula, the most ancient occultism of India, but never before written in a book, though handed down from Teacher to Pupil. Miss Sharpe has studied the works of the great Shankaracharya and her philosophy is both sincere and spontaneous, the outcome of many years' hard study. In her latest book we have a collection of philosophical aphorisms (the Tantras) and she treats of a mystical and occult philosophy. As she says, "the knower of precious things will know their value. Knowledge is inseparable from the knower."

In her introduction, the authoress tells us that she was recently given to read a secret treatise on mystic rites which are still being performed in occult societies, in both the East and the West. She says that the verses of the Tantras have been jealously guarded and recited for centuries by devout Indians.

> "There are no royal roads to God; except the old worn ways of sacrifice and austerity. The wearing of the ragged robe that hides kingliness; the blazoning out and following of old truths; . . . knitting Him throughout one's human body, till the will of man becomes automatically God's will; till the man and God are inextricably one; these are the only ways; this is the only goal; this the finality of human achievement."

Here are some notable excerpts from the book:

V.i. "There are three kinds of meditation: on sacred words; on an unmanifested God; and on a God with Divine attributes. 2. Devotion and service are the highest form of worship."

VV.i. "There is a nectar in the body of the Pure Virgin: to that comes the spirit incarnate. 2. The body of man is the universe in miniature."

IX.I. "He who worships with anger in his heart loses his merit; even as the water in the half baked pot loses itself. 2. Greed destroys all good qualities. 5. When in the process of meditation, the meditator and the object of meditation are merged, then arises the nectar of wisdom."

This little book of Miss Sharpe will be heartily received by the scholar and the philosopher and will meet with the warm approbation of both.